The Complete Guide to Scottish Terriers

Tracey Squaire

LP Media Inc. Publishing

Text copyright © 2019 by LP Media Inc.

All rights reserved.

No part of this book may be reproduced or transmitted in any form or by any means, electronic or mechanical, including photocopying, recording, or by an information storage and retrieval system - except by a reviewer who may quote brief passages in a review to be printed in a magazine or newspaper - without permission in writing from the publisher. For information address LP Media Inc. Publishing, 3178 253rd Ave. NW, Isanti, MN 55040

www.lpmedia.org

Publication Data

Scottish Terriers

The Complete Guide to Scottish Terriers ---- First edition.

Summary: "Successfully raising a Scottish Terrier dog from puppy to old age" --- Provided by publisher.

ISBN: 978-1-09669-607-0

[1. Scottish Terriers --- Non-Fiction] I. Title.

This book has been written with the published intent to provide accurate and authoritative information in regard to the subject matter included. While every reasonable precaution has been taken in preparation of this book the author and publisher expressly disclaim responsibility for any errors, omissions, or adverse effects arising from the use or application of the information contained inside. The techniques and suggestions are to be used at the reader's discretion and are not to be considered a substitute for professional veterinary care. If you suspect a medical problem with your dog, consult your veterinarian.

Design by Sorin Rădulescu

First paperback edition, 2019

TABLE OF CONTENTS

CHAPTER 1
Scottish Terrier History ... 8
What is a Scottish Terrier? ... 8
History of the Scottish Terrier ... 10
Physical Characteristics ... 13
Breed Behavioral Characteristics ... 14
Is a Scottish Terrier the Right Fit for You? ... 16

CHAPTER 2
Choosing a Scottish Terrier ... 18
Buying vs. Adopting ... 18
How to Find a Reputable Breeder ... 22
Researching Breeders ... 23
Health Tests and Certifications ... 26
Breeder Contracts and Guarantees ... 27
Choosing the Perfect Pup ... 27
Tips for Adopting a Scottish Terrier ... 29

CHAPTER 3
Preparing Your Home for Your Scottish Terrier ... 30
Helping Your Current Pets and Children Adapt ... 30
Dangerous Things that Dogs Might Eat ... 32
Other Household Dangers ... 33
Preparing a Space for Your Dog Inside ... 33
Preparing Outside Spaces ... 36

CHAPTER 4
Bringing Home Your Scottish Terrier ... 38
The Importance of Having a Plan ... 38
Pet Supplies to Have Ready ... 40
The Ride Home ... 42

The First Night Home 42
First Vet Visit/Choosing a Vet 43
Puppy Classes 44
Cost Breakdown for the First Year 45

CHAPTER 5
Being a Puppy Parent 48
Standing by Your Expectations 48
How to Crate Train 50
Bedtime 52
Chewing 53
Growling and Barking 54
Digging 55
Running Away 55
Separation Anxiety 56
Leaving Your Dog Home Alone 57

CHAPTER 6
House-Training 58
Different Options for Potty Training 58
The First Few Weeks 59
Rewarding Positive Behavior 60
Crate Training for House-Training Use 61
Playpens and Doggy Doors 63

CHAPTER 7
Socializing with People and Animals 64
Importance of Good Socialization 64
Behavior Around Other Dogs 66
Ways to Socialize Your Dog with Other Pets 67
Properly Greeting New People 69
Scottish Terriers and Children 69

CHAPTER 8
Scottish Terriers and Your Other Pets 70
Pack Mentality 70
Introducing Your New Puppy to the Other Pack Members ... 71
Raising Multiple Puppies from the Same Litter 73
Fighting/Bad Behavior 73

CHAPTER 9
Physical and Mental Exercise — 76
Exercise Requirements — 76
Different Types of Exercise to Try — 77
Importance of Mental Exercise — 81
Tips for Keeping Your Scottish Terrier Occupied — 82

CHAPTER 10
Clear Expectations — 84
Hiring a Trainer/Attending Classes — 87
Owner Behavior — 87
Operant Conditioning Basics — 89
Primary and Secondary Reinforcements — 91

CHAPTER 11
Basic Commands — 92
Benefits of Proper Training — 92
Picking the Right Rewards/Treats — 93
Different Training Methods — 95
    Positive Reinforcement — 95
    Mirror Training — 95
    Clicker Training — 95
    Pack Leader Training — 95
Relationship Training — 96
Basic Commands — 97
    Focus — 97
    Sit — 97
    Lie Down — 98
    Stay — 99
    Release — 99
    Come — 99
    Off/Down — 100
    Give/Drop — 100
    Walk/Heel — 100
    Advanced Commands — 101

CHAPTER 12
Dealing With Unwanted Behaviors — 102
Understanding Bad Behavior in Dogs — 102
Bad Behavior Prevention and Correction — 104
Scottish-Terrier-Specific Bad Habits — 107

CHAPTER 13
Traveling with Scottish Terriers — 108
Dog Carriers and Car Restraints — 108
Preparing Your Dog for Car Rides — 110
Packing and Preparing for a Car Ride — 111
Flying and Hotel Stays — 112
Kenneling vs. Dog Sitters — 113
Tips and Tricks for Traveling — 115

CHAPTER 14
Nutrition — 116
Importance of Good Diet — 116
Balanced Nutrition for Your Dog — 117
Signs and Symptoms of Improper Nutrition — 119
Good Foods for Scottish Terriers — 121
Different Types of Commercial Food for Small Dogs — 122
- Puppies — 122
- Adults — 122
- Seniors — 123

Feeding During Pregnancy — 124
Subscription Services, Homemade Foods, Recipes — 125
People Food – Harmful and Acceptable Kinds — 126
Weight Management — 126

CHAPTER 15
Grooming Your Scottish Terrier — 128
When Professional Help is Necessary — 129
Coat Basics — 130
Bathing and Brushing — 130
Trimming the Nails — 132
Brushing Their Teeth — 132
Cleaning Ears and Eyes — 133

CHAPTER 16
Basic Health Care — 134
Visiting the Vet — 134
Fleas and Ticks — 134
Worms and Parasites — 136
Holistic Alternatives — 136
Vaccinations — 138
Pet Insurance — 139

CHAPTER 17
Advanced Scottish Terrier Health and Aging Dog Care   **140**
Common Diseases, Conditions, and Genetic Traits in Scottish Terriers **140**
Illness and Injury Prevention **144**
Basics of Senior Dog Care **145**
Common Old-age Ailments **146**
Grooming **148**
Nutrition **148**
Exercise **149**
When It's Time to Say Goodbye **149**

CHAPTER 1
Scottish Terrier History

What is a Scottish Terrier?

A close cousin to the West Highland White Terrier, the Scottish Terrier, fondly known as the Scottie, is a breed of terrier that is best known for its spirited and sometimes-serious nature. Though this dog grows no taller than about 10 inches, the Scottish Terrier is widely thought to be a big dog in a small dog's body. With the energy of a small dog and the audacity of a large dog, the Scottie is well-known for its work ethic, watchful eye for strangers, and graceful demeanor.

This breed is as proud of itself as its owners are of the breed. Scotties are not for the lenient pet owner. Scottish Terriers are confident and may revolt if not trained with a strong but kind hand. Scottish Terriers have a strong will, but they are loyal and affectionate to their families, especially if their family consists of one or two human adults.

Scottish Terriers differ from other Terriers in that they're far more independent than most Terriers and need a reason to follow directions. Scotties take themselves very seriously both on and off the show stage and easily adapt to new environments and new experiences with confidence. This breed loves fun and excitement and will add both to the lives of its owners.

HELPFUL TIP
Kings and Queens

The Scottish Terrier was bred to burrow and hunt small vermin in the hills of Scotland. In the 17th century, King James VI of Scotland owned one of these strong-willed, fierce, and brave little dogs. So smitten was he by the breed that he sent six Scotties to France as a gift to the nobility. Later, Queen Victoria of England kept her kennel stocked with Scotties. Her favorite was named "Laddie."

Highly affectionate and highly intelligent, it really is no wonder that this adaptable watchdog has reached an iconic status among dog lovers and remained popular in America for generations. Whether as work dogs, companions, or hunters, the businesslike and bold demeanor of Scottish Terriers makes them the perfect dog breed choice for anyone looking for an independent companion.

CHAPTER 1 Scottish Terrier History

Photo Courtesy of Ann Marie French

History of the Scottish Terrier

Originally bred and raised to track down and eliminate farm vermin, Scottish Terriers have long protected humans from intruders and been loyal members of the family. Even the Romans admired this breed and named them "workers of the earth." Today, their nickname is "little diehard," and though all of these bearded hunters are no longer searching out badgers, foxes, weasels, rats, and other farm vermin in the Highlands of Scotland, Scottish Terriers haven't lost the dutiful and fearless watchfulness that makes them so popular as farm dogs and hunting companions.

The actual origin of the Scottish Terrier is unknown, but the first record of a dog matching the description of this breed was discovered in a book titled The History of Scotland 1436-1561. Almost 200 years after that mention, Scottish King James VI became English King James I, inadvertently prompting the widespread breeding of the Scotties we know today. By gifting six of his beloved Terriers to a French monarch, King James made the world aware of the Terrier breed that would go on to become the Scottish Terrier.

CHAPTER 1 Scottish Terrier History

The specific Terrier breeds we know today weren't so well defined in the 19th century, especially on the Isle of Skye where generically-named Terriers roamed and were abundant. Since so many different breeds inhabited the area, most were clumped together into one group named Skye Terriers. The breed that is now the Scottish Terrier was among those generically named Terriers.

> *"All dogs are good; any terrier is better; a Scottie is best."*
> — Francis G. Lloyd

Before being featured in and winning several dog shows, the Scottish Terrier had not been widely considered a good animal companion; the ancestor of this breed was not very social and not very friendly, meaning breeders, strangers, and other animals suffered many bites during encounters with this fierce watchdog.

Once dog shows started becoming more popular in England, the Scottish Terrier breed became defined so judges could compare contestants to a set breed standard, and its popularity increased. Other popular breeds that stemmed from the generic "Skye Terrier" breed include the current Skye Terrier, the West Highland White Terrier, and the Cairn Terrier.

At this point in the breed's history, there is little information lost to inattention or uncaring; the names of many of the dogs who helped create the standard Scottie today are recorded and celebrated in history for all to see.

Several early dog-show winners are said to be the source of all Scottish Terrier pedigrees, and the breeders of those dogs spread the award-winning genes of their regal companions far. After both England and Scotland established their own Scottish Terrier dog clubs and set different official breed standards, the breed's standard had to become even more defined. Eventually, the standard characteristics of Scottish Terriers were based on the look of four dogs and their offspring who are responsible for the head length, short stature, and square body this Terrier now boasts.

In the early 1890s, the Scottish Terrier was introduced in America, and a few years after, America established its own Scottish Terrier dog club. Three different American presidents have claimed the Scottish Terrier among their family members while in office, making the Scottish Terrier the only breed to have lived within the White House three times. Today, the Scottie remains among the more popular animal companions in America.

Physical Characteristics

The modern Scottie can be best recognized by its perky ears, regal profile, and water-resistant outer coat. This pup's fur mostly comes in black, brindle, or a wheaten color; white is the only color this breed will not come in, though you will often find white strands mixed in with the other fur colors.

The Scottie's fur lends a lot to its distinctive appearance. With two different layers of fur making up its coat, this pup may look slightly bigger than it really is. The Scottie's undercoat is dense enough to resist water, and the outer coat is actually hair and boasts wiry long strands that grow about two inches in length. Its long and shaggy hair forms a beard and bushy eyebrows, making this Terrier seem aloof and standoffish, which you may definitely desire in a watchdog.

At only 18-22 pounds, this small breed packs a lot of power into its compact and sturdy form. The Scottish Terrier's short stature and heavy bones gives this energetic dog the power it needs to protect your home if needed. Though their furry legs are tiny, Scottish Terriers have powerful legs designed for digging, and they do enjoy digging, so make sure your yard is ready to contain this escape artist. Though Scottie legs are strong, the breed doesn't do well running; a walk around the neighborhood will be enough to work those tiny legs.

Scottish Terrier heights range between 25.5 to 28 cm, or 10 to 11 inches. Males typically weigh between 19 and 22 pounds while females typically weigh between 18 and 21 pounds. The Scottish Terriers responsible for the breed's current appearance are Heather Necessity, Albourne Barty, Albourne Annie Laurie, and Marksman of Docken, regal names for those who modified the standard of Scottish Terriers. These four contributed the square body, the head length, and short legs that can be seen in the breed today. With such a strong ancestry, you can be confident that no matter the gender, the size, or the coloring of your Scottish Terrier, he or she will be fiercely loyal to you and will protect both you and your home.

Breed Behavioral Characteristics

"Scotties are known for having a fierce loyalty, their independence, intelligence, diehard mentality, and occasional stubbornness. Scotties do things on their own time, if they want to do it at all."

Jane Herron
Herron's Sandhills Scotties

The Scottish Terrier is highly independent and, therefore, may sometimes seem stubborn. Along with being independent, this breed is also intelligent, so training sessions may be frustrating, but persistence and diverse teaching methods are sure to keep your Scottie displaying good, non-aggressive behaviors. Since the Scottie is so intelligent, he responds well to verbal praise and chastisement; your Scottie will know when you're upset with him just by the tone of your voice, so use that power thoughtfully.

Scottish Terriers also tend to be sensitive, and their personalities can be very distinct at times as they display their opinionated nature. Be careful about how you treat your Scottish Terrier and what you say around him as he will know you're talking about him and won't take kindly if he's being made fun of.

Despite this breed's small size, its bark is hardy and will serve as a proper warning for vermin and intruders alike to stay away from your yard. But if you live in an apartment or another area in which a watchful pup barking at every passerby isn't acceptable, a Scottish Terrier may be a bad idea. Scottish Terriers are territorial and enjoy patrolling the home both inside and out.

Scottish Terriers are not needy dogs and won't be content without their own space and their own "me" time. They consider themselves to be part of a pack instead of a pet in a family; treat your Scottie like a companion, and you'll be rewarded with life-long loyalty.

While Scotties can certainly tolerate being alone and won't typically suffer from separation anxiety, they enjoy being with their families and can be incredibly affectionate toward a chosen few if not just one person. If the Scottie is properly socialized early on, you will have no problem ensuring your pup is friendly toward children and other animals. Without early socialization, the Scottish Terrier can and will be grumpy with other dogs and with children. Scottish Terriers weren't bred to be friendly with other ani-

CHAPTER 1 Scottish Terrier History

Photo Courtesy of Debbie Jones

mals, but they typically wait to be provoked before acting. The Scottie is not afraid to give a warning nip or bark to an annoying or disrespectful child or animal, so socialize early and often.

Scottish Terriers have a tendency to wander around as they were bred for hunting vermin in the Scottish Highlands, so they'll keep your yard pest free, but they're also likely to go chasing a squirrel, cat, or other moving objects; proper fencing will keep both your pet and the neighborhood animals safe.

Is a Scottish Terrier the Right Fit for You?

Now that you know all about this regal companion and its long history, you must decide if the Scottish Terrier is the right dog breed for you. While most dogs can adapt to the lifestyles of humans, it's easier on both you and the pup if you choose a breed whose character already fits your lifestyle.

In regard to the Scottish Terrier, you must keep in mind that this breed needs to be part of a family; while the Scottie doesn't do well with kids and other animals without proper socialization, it still wants to be part of a pack. Adult humans are the best companions for Scottish Terriers. Scottish Terriers have a high level of energy, but they aren't marathon runners. They need a moderate amount of daily exercise and are not content to sit and relax at your feet constantly (though that is an activity you can both enjoy together!).

Consider the characteristics of this breed and ask yourself a few questions to figure out if the Scottish Terrier is right for your lifestyle. Think about if you're prepared to own a small dog with the personality of a big dog. Imagine how big dogs still think they're puppies and think about the opposite: a small pup acting fiercely unafraid of anything. That kind of dog

Photo Courtesy of Cheryl Fugate

may not be right for you if you have other pets who may be aggressive; Scotties are warriors and aren't afraid of a fight!

Scottish Terriers will follow their instincts to chase and dig and kill small animals. This is something you need to keep in mind if you don't have a properly fenced yard, own other small animals, or have a problem with having the occasional hole in your backyard. You can, of course, train your pup to prevent these problems, so make sure you're ready for some stern but fair training.

Again, the Scottish Terrier is an independent warrior with a strong personality, and to keep your little warrior strong and healthy, you'll need to participate in daily brisk walks; if you're not prepared to give the Scottie the exercise it needs, perhaps a lapdog is better suited to your lifestyle.

The Scottish Terrier also requires a good bit of grooming; it's no wonder with the length of its outer coat, and to keep your Scottie looking fresh and regal, you either need to be dedicated to grooming one to three times a week or be able to afford to take your Scottie to a groomer periodically.

The Scottish Terrier is a good addition to the safety-focused family and a perfect fit for those living a solitary lifestyle. While this breed can certainly be personable and energetic, the Scottish Terrier may not be the best companion to young children. This compact but high-spirited breed is a great choice for those looking to fill their small-spaced home with a lot of personality.

CHAPTER 2
Choosing a Scottish Terrier

Buying vs. Adopting

HELPFUL TIP: Puppy or Rescue?

The Scottish Terrier Club of America (stca.biz) is a great place to begin your search for a rescue coordinator in your area. Not all rescue dogs adapt easily to new homes, however. A reputable organization member will make a home visit to assess if the family and home is suitable for the dog. Expect to pay an adoption fee to help defer the cost of medical bills, grooming, and food during the foster period.

As with most animals, adopting will be the least expensive method of bringing a new Scottish Terrier into your life, but price is not always the primary concern when deciding whether to bring a new companion into your life.

Adopting a Scottish Terrier will run you around $300 while, depending on the breeder, buying a Scottish Terrier can cost upward of $2,000. That price difference is nothing to sniff about, but if money is no object to you, you may consider adopting because you'll be giving a pet a loving home.

Besides the fact that you can give a homeless pet a loving family, adopting a Scottie may be your preference if you want to guarantee the personality of your new pet; rescue center workers learn the personality of the animals they work with and can let you know if the Scottish Terrier you're interested in will play nice with your other pets. Many Scottish Terriers are given up because of aggression issues and require proper training that will be harder to implement than if the dog had been trained correctly while young. Others have no problems and end up in shelters for various reasons.

Adoption centers also offer more diversity with breed mixes. The Scottish Terrier key characteristics stand out even when mixed in with other breeds, and when adopting a mixed breed, you gain the benefits from the other breeds. Here are some popular Scottie mixes:

CHAPTER 2   Choosing a Scottish Terrier

Photo Courtesy of
Claudia Granados

Photo Courtesy of Amanda Vearnals

CHAPTER 2   Choosing a Scottish Terrier

- The Scorkie (Scottish Terrier and Yorkshire Terrier)
- The Pugottie (Scottish Terrier and Pug)
- The Scoodle (Scottish Terrier and Poodle)
- The Bascottie (Scottish Terrier and Basset Hound)
- The Sceagle (Scottish Terrier and Beagle)
- The Scolden Terrier (Scottish Terrier and Golden Retriever)
- The Scottese (Scottish Terrier and Maltese)
- And more!

Even though there are Scotties and Scottish Terrier mixes for adoption, you may have a hard time actually finding them near you. Scottish Terriers are very popular dogs, and even adoption and rescue centers specifically for Scottish Terriers may not have a pup for adoption. A quick search around your area will let you know if there's one such rescue near you.

Choosing to buy a Scottie also won't guarantee that you'll get one; breeders like to ensure the pups they raise go to loving families, and they also often have a long waiting list for buyers. Scottish Terriers don't welp large litters, so demand is high for this companion.

Reputable breeders will provide a health history for any pets you buy from them, something you may not get from adoption. Having the health history of the family line and testing done for health problems can keep you from experiencing heartache and large vet bills later in life. Reputable breeders go the extra mile to ensure that the lines they breed are free of inherited conditions. Lastly, you may have to travel across the country to actually find a reputable Scottish Terrier breeder, whereas you may find one in a local shelter if you're lucky.

Either way, if you decide to add a Scottish Terrier to your life, you will be giving a loving home to a sweet and loyal dog.

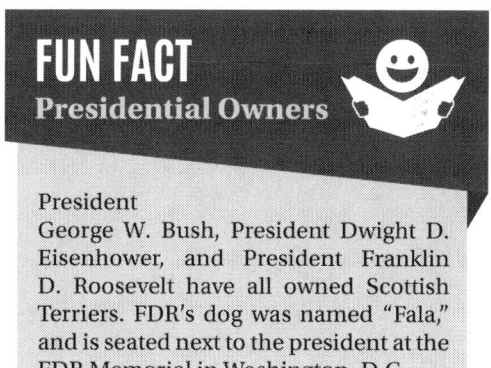

FUN FACT
Presidential Owners

President George W. Bush, President Dwight D. Eisenhower, and President Franklin D. Roosevelt have all owned Scottish Terriers. FDR's dog was named "Fala," and is seated next to the president at the FDR Memorial in Washington, D.C.

How to Find a Reputable Breeder

Photo Courtesy of Ambre Bethoux and Jake Wehner

The breeder you choose depends on what kind of Scottish Terrier you're looking for. Many breeders can be found by attending dog shows. Some breeders specialize in agility, while others specialize in obedience and even more. If you have a specific reason for adopting a Scottish Terrier other than just wanting to own one of these iconic dogs, pay attention to the breeders at dog shows, and speak with the trainers themselves to get recommendations on reputable breeders.

Another place to search for reputable breeders is the American Kennel Club (AKC) website. Since breeders who claim that their dogs are purebred must have evidence of such, you can search the AKC website to find if a dog is registered. The website also has an area for breeder referrals. According to the AKC website, the AKC acknowledges breeders who "demonstrate a commitment to the AKC community, dedication to their breeds, and actively support the sport of purebred dogs." Additionally, breeders can earn a certificate indicating that they have met specific testing standards as well as continue their education on healthy breeding.

The first two options are the best ways to find reputable breeders, but of course you can simply do a web search for reputable breeders. Many breeders may have websites that list not only their currently available pups but also their previous litters, the dams and sires that produced each litter, any awards that their lines have won, and more. Different breeders have different information available.

CHAPTER 2 Choosing a Scottish Terrier

Researching Breeders

"It's very important to see how your breeder will raise your puppy. Is the puppy in a kennel? If the puppy is in a kennel, who's watching the puppies? Who's guaranteeing you a temperament you can stand behind? I prefer to buy my Scottie's from those who raise them as family, whether they are a pet or a show animal."

Lainie Culton
Culton's Scottish Terriers

Even if you've gotten a recommendation for a breeder from someone you trust, you want to do your own research before buying from anyone. This is especially true if you've found a breeder online; research is important to not only ensure that the breeder isn't really a puppy mill in disguise but also so you know that the breeder is responsible and doesn't overbreed or breed sick animals. It's the responsibility of the breeder and the buyer to stop harmful breeding practices that produce sickly puppies all across the country.

To research your breeder, start with the internet. It's the easiest way to research many breeders at once before narrowing your choices. There are many breeders and many people who call themselves breeders, so you can and should be picky about where you get your Scottish Terrier.

A good place to start your online research is the Scottish Terrier Club of America (STCA) website which can be found on the main AKC website along with a list of all the parent clubs under the AKC. The AKC parent clubs have lists of reputable breeders for their specific breeds. Breeders on these lists are expected to follow the code of ethics put forth by each club. These breeders are dedicated to the health and future of their respective breeds.

Speak with multiple dog breeders before settling on a breeder. You'll begin to get a sense of common practices among reputable breeders. For instance, reputable breeders typically choose one or two breeds not only to breed but also to learn as much as possible about. A reputable breeder should also be passionate about the dogs they breed. Talking with multiple breeders will help you get a sense of which breeders you can trust to be reputable. If you know a breeder for, say, Beagles even

Tracey SQUAIRE | The Complete Guide to Scottish Terriers

Photo Courtesy of Amanda Hodgson

though you're looking for a Scottish Terrier breeder, the Beagle breeder may know someone who has the breed you desire. After all, breeders who are passionate about what they do tend to congregate with other passionate breeders.

You'll want to visit the place where your prospective new puppy was bred, born, and raised. There are a few things you'll want to see during your visit. First of all, you need to see one or both of the puppy parents, specifically the mother because puppies shouldn't be separated from their mothers before eight weeks of age. If a breeder insists that you take a pup before it is eight weeks old, leave that breeder's facility; he or she is not responsible or does not care about the health of the dogs they breed. Puppies who are removed from their mothers and siblings too early in order for the breeder to sell as many puppies in as short a time as possible bear the weight of that greed and often deal with lifelong psychological, behavioral, and emotional problems, and as the owner of such a puppy, you will also be living with these problems. A puppy is not a human child, so it's important that you remember you cannot provide the emotional and social support that a puppy younger than eight weeks needs in order to be healthy.

Walk around the breeder's facility and inspect it for cleanliness and bad odors. Dogs should have access to clean living areas, clean water, and an open and friendly environment. You'll want to get a sense of the health of the dogs living there. Do the animals all look well-fed? Are they coughing or do they have runny noses or eyes? Oftentimes, puppies do not immediately display illnesses contracted and inherited because of irresponsible breeders. The breeder should be upfront with you about any illnesses or diseases affecting the breed as a whole, and the dogs they raise should be comfortable and friendly around both you and the breeder.

Reputable breeders expect you to ask questions because they want to make sure the puppies they sell are going to good homes, and a reputable breeder shouldn't mind being asked questions about the dogs they breed.

Health Tests and Certifications

Reputable breeders should have certificates indicating that the Scottish Terriers they're breeding are free from the common genetic disorders found within the breed.

Breeders must have their breeding lines tested for Von Willebrand's disease, a disorder that humans share with dogs which is caused by a missing or defective clotting protein. Those who suffer from this disorder may experience major bleeding from even the smallest of wounds. With your fierce and fearless Scottie dutifully patrolling your territory every chance she gets, you can be sure that she'll incur a scratch or two either from the environment or the other animals living there. This disorder can cause death as uncontrollable bleeding can occur in some cases. Bleeding can be both excessive and prolonged.

According to the STCA, "Treatment of von Willebrand's involves intravenous infusion of fresh whole blood or plasma, at 3-5 ml/lb, with topical use of blood clotting compounds, and avoidance of drugs that interfere with blood clotting." This disorder cannot be cured, and it costs between $500 and $1,000 to treat the results of the disorder with a blood transfusion after a traumatic injury or unexpected complication during surgery. That estimate is for just one treatment, and some dogs or puppies may require multiple transfusions in order to restore normal blood levels.

Breeders must also have a patella evaluation done to ensure that the line does not suffer from patellar luxation, an orthopedic condition that occurs frequently in Scottish Terriers, other small dogs, and some larger breeds. Patellar luxation occurs when the patella (or the knee cap) moves out of its natural position. This condition is incredibly painful, can lead to lameness, and is guaranteed to eventually rupture the dog's cranial cruciate ligament (an important stabilizer inside the canine knee joint). The cost to treat this condition ranges from $1,500 to $3,000.

Your chosen reputable breeder can show you a Little Registration that shows that his or her puppies meet the AKC breed standards. You should also receive a certificate for your puppy indicating that they are, indeed, registered and eligible to compete in AKC events.

Your breeder may also have a certificate from the AKC indicating that he or she is a Breeder of Merit, a purebred dog breeder who goes "above and beyond on health issues, temperament, and genetic screening, as well as to the individual care and placement of puppies in responsible homes." Many breeders also boast a H.E.A.R.T. certificate which shows that they have educated themselves on breeding best practices.

CHAPTER 2   Choosing a Scottish Terrier

Breeder Contracts and Guarantees

Your breeder should present you with a contract. This contract acts as a bill of sale as well as an outline of both your rights as a buyer and the breeder's rights as a seller. This contract may guarantee many claims by the breeder and many rights for you as the buyer. For instance, many breeders will allow you to return a puppy within three years of a sale if that puppy happens to display any genetic disorder covered within the contract. Your breeder may also include in the contract that you are required to spay or neuter your pet.

What your puppy sale contract includes depends on what reputable breeder you choose to purchase your pup from. Read carefully before agreeing to the contract and taking home your new family member.

Choosing the Perfect Pup

"We recommend looking for a Scottie that has a docile temperament, and will come and engage you with play. Friendliness and alertness are also good signs."

Jane Herron
Herron's Sandhills Scotties

The perfect pup doesn't exist, but there IS a perfect pup for you and your family, and the only way to discover which puppy of the litter fits you and your family's lifestyle is to spend as much time as possible with the litter before taking home your new family member.

You first need to understand the personality and temperament of the breed; Scotties can adjust to pretty much any living environment and don't need a ton of exercise besides a daily walk, but when you're interacting with puppies before taking one home, try to find a pup whose energy levels seem to match your lifestyle. Even though breeds have certain characteristics, each dog is an individual and will have his or her own personality.

Before taking home my Beagle as a puppy, my household had considered another dog, some type of Husky mix; she was beautiful and happy to see us and oh so energetic. We loved her the moment we saw her and for fifteen minutes after. But during our short time with her, she chewed on everything she came into contact with. She peed several times from excitement and was just overall much to energetic for my household. It really is vital to spend as much time with an animal as possible before taking them home because I now know that neither I nor that sweet girl would have been happy if I'd taken her home with me. My Beagle, Arthur, is still energetic, and he loves chewing as well, but once he burns off his energy, he's very calm and will gladly lie in my lap or nearby as I write or edit or enjoy being inside. Choose the pup for your lifestyle, not just the one who captures your attention the most.

Scottish Terriers are generally fearless, but you may find a shy puppy who doesn't want to stray far from his mother. Consider if you want a pup who is likely to stick closer to you than others; Scotties are already very loyal, but they are also independent and don't need your company or attention, even if they enjoy and appreciate it. If you're looking for independence, you don't want the needy pup, but if you're looking for comfort from a creature who needs you as much as you need them, bond with the puppy who loves his mama too much and make sure you're prepared to give him the love he wants and needs.

Of course, behavior is not always the only reason to choose a pup. If you're considering entering your Scottish Terrier into dog shows, your breeder will likely have a few "show picks" that match the temperament and physical standards judges look for in the breed.

Many breeders may offer to choose a puppy for you after observing your interactions with the litter. Breeders have years of experience finding homes for their litters, and they can usually tell which of their puppies will go with your lifestyle, as long as you and your breeder are communicating and learning about each other as you should be. Remember that breeders want to ensure the puppies they breed go to good homes. Reputable breeders truly care about the dogs they breed, and many of them consider their dogs to be part of their families.

Tips for Adopting a Scottish Terrier

"Remember 'rescue' does not mean sick, broken inside, or damaged. It means the family that had me first did not know my breed or how to handle me, so I suffered for that. Be patient and loving to your rescue because Scottie's are strong and adaptable."

Lainie Culton
Culton's Scottish Terriers

Adopting should be an option for you only if you're prepared to deal with the problems that some irresponsible owners cause by not properly training or socializing their animals. Many dogs, regardless of breed, are given up for adoption because of behavioral issues, so when you adopt a Scottish Terrier, you must be prepared to do extra training not only to properly teach the Scottie how to live amongst humans but also to unteach it the negative behaviors it may have learned in its previous home.

Some behavioral problems you may notice in an adopted Scottish Terrier include a short temper, greediness or possessiveness, aggressiveness toward other animals or children, and inconsistent house-training. These problems are usually the fault of the previous owners. Scottish Terriers must be properly socialized early on and require consistent and clear training in order to display positive behaviors.

Besides behavioral problems, there are also Scotties who were given up because of the tragedies of life; Scottish Terriers are great companions for older people or for people who live alone, so, unfortunately, once such people pass or can no longer care for their beloved pet, that pet is given to a shelter. Scotties in this situation have likely lost someone they considered a lifelong companion; Scottish Terriers often bond with just one or two people, so you will need to spend a lot of time gaining the trust of an adopted Scottish Terrier. You may never attain the same relationship with an adopted Scottie that he had with its previous owner, but you WILL be giving a lonely and sad creature a place to call home. Remember that when you bring an animal into your life you are doing so for selfish reasons, but also remember that you can bring kindness and happiness to others through this particular act of selfishness.

CHAPTER 3
Preparing Your Home for Your Scottish Terrier

Helping Your Current Pets and Children Adapt

If you already have pets and children in your household, good! You can start socializing your Scottish Terrier early. Scottish Terriers aren't known to get along with other animals and with children, but teaching your animals and children how to respectfully interact with each other can help change that.

Before bringing home your Scottish Terrier, make sure everyone in your home not only knows that someone new is coming but also knows how to interact with that someone new. For instance, if you have other pets, bring something home that smells like your new Scottie to get the old pets used to the scent of the new dog. If your pets are the excitable or intrusive type, consider leashing them for the initial meeting; Scottish Terriers aren't afraid to show their annoyance, but no puppy deserves to be overwhelmed its first day in a new home. The same goes for children: make sure they know the rules about interacting with animals respectfully. Warn them that even if they're used to other dogs, the Scottie won't take poking or prodding lightly.

Your current pets may become territorial during the first meeting, so before you bring home the new pup, put anyway anything that belongs specifically to any of the current pets including beds, favorite toys, and food/water bowls. Make sure the space you plan to introduce the animals in is clean and open enough so no one feels confined or too close. You may even consider introducing the animals in a neutral area outside or away from the home.

Children should know that a new puppy isn't a plaything, it's a living being. Teach your children to be calm and patient in their interactions with the new dog, and warn them that they may need to wait until the new dog has adjusted to his new environment before approaching. Your Scottish Terrier should be allowed to approach his new family members in his own time.

It may be wise to share the history of the Scottish Terrier with any children in the household. They may find it interesting, and stories of fierce Scottie warriors may serve as all the warning you need to ensure everyone remains respectful around this small-game hunter.

CHAPTER 3   Preparing Your Home for Your Scottish Terrier

Photo Courtesy of Carol White

Dangerous Things that Dogs Might Eat

There are many foods that are dangerous for dogs to consume for various reasons. Though dogs are made to eat meat, the way humans store meat may lead to illnesses. Many natural foods such as fruits, vegetables, and nuts can cause negative reactions if consumed. Additionally, many of the chemicals in the foods we eat are harmful to dogs. To keep your dog safe and healthy, keep the following food products away from your Scottish Terrier.

FOOD	LEADS TO
Chocolate	Seizures, vomiting, diarrhea, uncontrolled urination (potentially fatal)
Macadamia nuts	Lethargy, vomiting, fever, tremors
Food items containing the sweetener Xylitol (diet foods, store-bought baked goods, candy, gum, etc.)	Liver failure, vomiting, increased heart rate, seizures
Onions, garlic, other alliums	Anemia, potentially fatal
Grapes and raisins	Kidney failure, lethargy, dehydration, vomiting, diarrhea
Anything containing nutmeg (pies, cakes, cookies)	Increased heart rate, dry mouth, seizures, stomach pain, disorientation
All parts of the avocado plant including the fruit, bark, stems, and leaves	Vomiting and diarrhea; fatal in large quantities
Mishandled raw meat	Diarrhea, vomiting, abdominal pain
Lemons and limes	Vomiting, diarrhea
Chicken bones	Bleeding, vomiting, drooling, moving oddly

Dogs may also get into some of the things we drink. Your Scottish Terrier should drink nothing but water (unless approved by your veterinarian), but the following drinks can be harmful to your Scottie.

DRINKS	LEADS TO
Coffee and tea	Seizures, vomiting, diarrhea, uncontrolled urination, potentially fatal
Any caffeinated soft drink	Seizures, vomiting, diarrhea,
Alcohol	Lethargy, vomiting, shortness of breath/panting
Saltwater	Vomiting, diarrhea, tremors, seizures

CHAPTER 3   Preparing Your Home for Your Scottish Terrier

Other Household Dangers

Food and drinks are harder to keep away from our animals, especially since they can be sneaky, but there are other household dangerous that can harm your Scottie if not properly stored or put out of reach. These items include medications of any kind for any species, pesticides or insecticides, fertilizers, antifreeze, deicer, oil, paint, paint thinner, batteries, power cords, bleach, and other household cleaners. These items are all around our homes, and it's important to keep them out of reach of your dog.

Preparing a Space for Your Dog Inside

Before you bring home your new Scottish Terrier, be sure to prepare a space inside that he can call his own, especially if there are already other pets in the home who have marked their territory.

Your Scottie needs a place for his kennel (if you choose to use a kennel), a place for his toys, and a place outside of his kennel to relax. Additionally, if you're bringing home a puppy who isn't yet house-trained, you will need a place to put newspaper or puppy pads.

Photo Courtesy of Sean and Chris Pugh

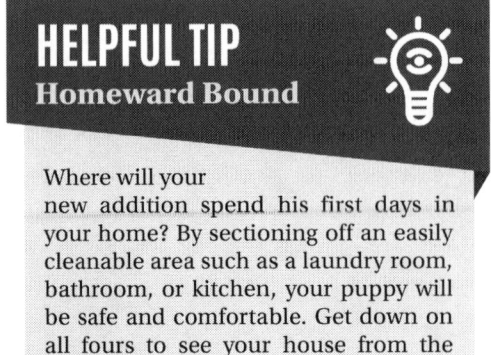

HELPFUL TIP
Homeward Bound

Where will your new addition spend his first days in your home? By sectioning off an easily cleanable area such as a laundry room, bathroom, or kitchen, your puppy will be safe and comfortable. Get down on all fours to see your house from the new dog's perspective. Watch for cords, wires, plants, and tablecloths. Remove all temptations prior to a mishap.

A good place to put a dog's kennel when first bringing it home is somewhere near where the rest of the family spends a lot of time. Dogs are social animals and want to feel as if they're part of the pack. If you put the kennel somewhere far away from the family's daily activities, your Scottie may feel isolated and alone. If your Scottie does seem overwhelmed when you first bring him home, place his kennel in a closed-off area such as a bedroom or laundry room, but make sure he has free access to enter and leave that area.

Puppy pads and newspapers should also go inside of laundry rooms or in an appropriate corner in the public area. Wherever you place these items must be somewhere easily and quickly accessible; puppy pads allow you to train your puppy to eliminate in appropriate areas.

Toys should be in a few different areas. If you don't make a plan for your Scottie's toys, they will sit where he leaves them after playtime. I personally prefer an open storage container that my dog can retrieve toys from at will. This container is in our main living area, but I also store toys inside of his kennel which is in one of the bedrooms. Dogs don't just live in one area, and their toys will travel as they do, but having one or two places in your home you know you can store toys will keep your home clean and your dog feeling as if he belongs. Trust me when I say that it will please your pup to see a container out in the open full of HIS stuff and covered in HIS scent.

Lastly, your Scottish Terrier needs somewhere outside of his kennel to live and be a dog. Dogs will often find a favorite place in your home for themselves, but if your dog is contending with other pets for prime real estate, you may consider outlining a specific area for your pup by placing a blanket with his scent along with some toys in the designated area. Scottish Terriers like to be near windows and other places they can observe their territories, so keep that in mind when hunting for the perfect relaxation station in your home.

CHAPTER 3 Preparing Your Home for Your Scottish Terrier

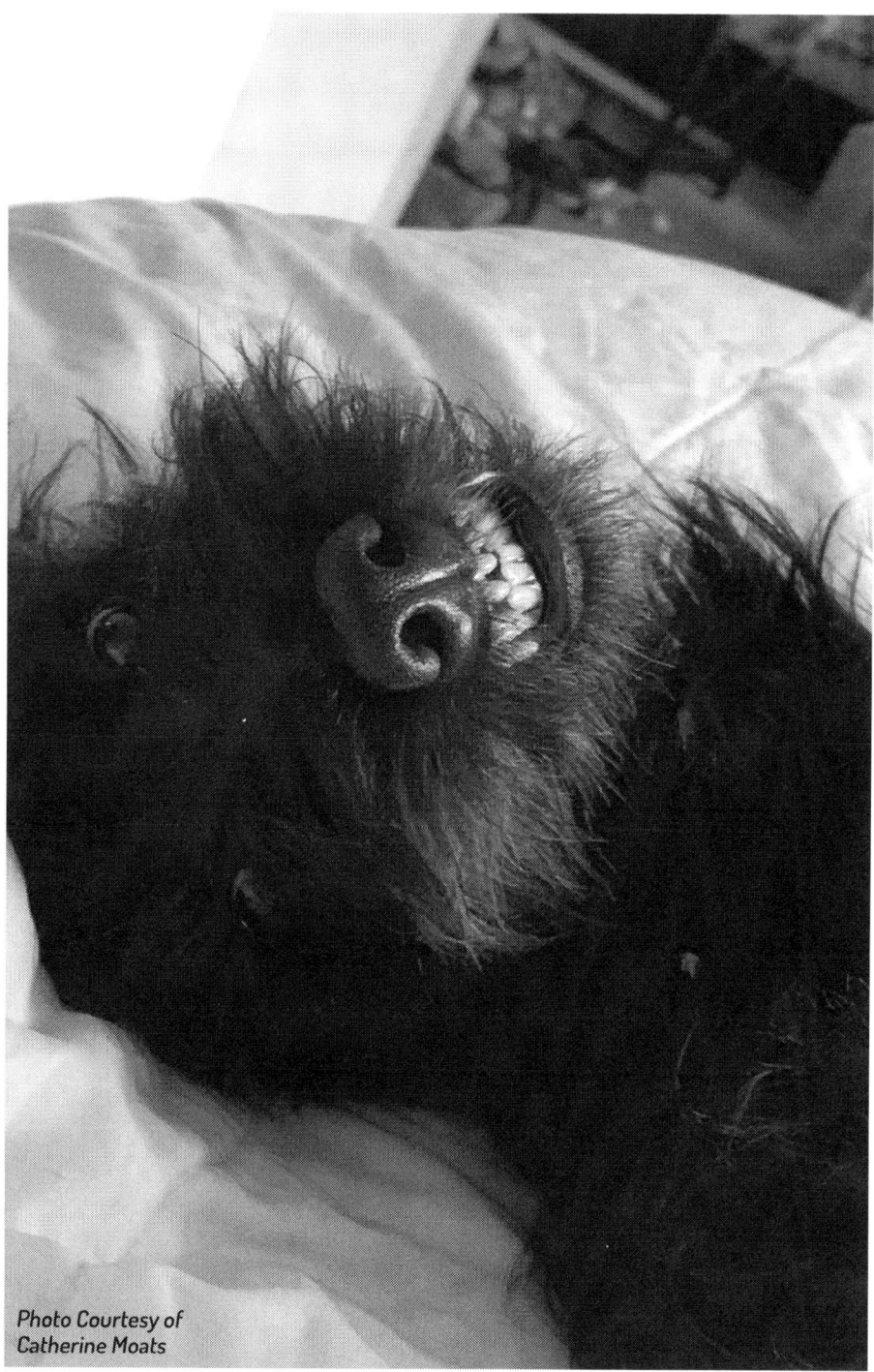

Photo Courtesy of Catherine Moats

Photo Courtesy of Emily Ashworth

Preparing Outside Spaces

Outside spaces are just as important as inside spaces, maybe even more so for Scotties. Inside of your home, your Scottie may feel more confident that all is well within his territory, but outside, he may be more on alert and, therefore, more likely to cause problems outside.

It is an absolute must to have a fenced yard if you plan to leave your Scottie outside unattended for any amount of time. Electric fences are not a safe option for this breed not only because other animals are not deterred by this technology but also because Scottish Terriers are fearless enough to run right through the border of an electric fence in order to chase a perceived intruder or hunt down small neighborhood animals. Many owners have, unfortunately, discovered this lesson for themselves after discovering their beloved friend missing or injured after escaping the yard.

With your yard safely fenced, you'll easily be able to outline different areas for your Scottie to perform various activities. The first area you need to outline is a potty area. I don't recommend letting your pup have free rein to eliminate anywhere in the yard, not even if the yard goes unused by the rest of the family. It's much more sanitary if your dog uses one area to do his business. Outline this area before you bring your pup home because you'll be walking or carrying him there during his housebreaking period.

Scottish Terriers love to dig, so it's a good idea to assign an area where that's permitted. If you don't make appropriate digging areas clear, your Scottie may dig up your garden or dig under your gate. There are many creative options for dog digging areas, depending on your preferences.

It's a good idea to outline a play area as well, especially if your family uses the yard often and you have stored items you don't want your pup to get into. This play area should have some sort of shade and access to clean water since your pup is sure to work up a thirst while digging or running around.

Be sure that your Scottish Terrier doesn't have access to the feces of other animals. Some dogs will eat cat feces if given the chance, and the feces of any animal, wild or domesticated, may pass on parasites or other diseases that can infect your dog just through contact. The same is true of any animal carcasses that your Scottie either discovers or creates himself. If your yard borders on any kind of wilderness, you may need to take further precautions like treating your yard for pests or pushing back the wilderness to keep wild animals away.

CHAPTER 4
Bringing Home Your Scottish Terrier

The Importance of Having a Plan

There's a reason prospective new parents spend months planning for the arrival of a new baby: no one wants to be scrambling to gather supplies and prepare an appropriate areas after a new responsibility has entered the home, so follow the lead of anxious new parents everywhere and make a plan for bringing home your Scottish Terrier.

Having a plan will cut down on a lot of stress with the ride home, first introductions, safe explorations, and more.

You should have a plan for how to introduce your Scottie to the other animals and children in your home. Consider practicing where everyone will stand and how they will act if your children happen to be excitable. Remember that this precaution is for everyone's safety. If you want to start the family bonding process early, ensure you have treats for the family to respectfully offer to the new family member.

I also recommend already having a potty schedule planned. Puppies don't have large bladders and will need to use the potty at consistent times, and having a schedule will make the house-training process much quicker and much less stressful. You should have fewer accidents if you're following a schedule, and if you prepare the schedule ahead of time, you can get a head start on the whole process. Your pup should go to the potty as soon as possible after arriving in her new home.

You'll also want to predetermine who the primary caretaker of your Scottie will be. Scottish Terriers typically bond with only one or two people, so consider this before bringing home your pup. Is the new dog specifically supposed to be a companion for someone? This person should be taking an active part in training, feeding, and socializing your Scottish Terrier.

Also be sure that everyone in the household understands the unique personality of the Scottish Terrier as well as the rules for interacting and living with your Scottie. Plans don't always go the way we expect, but having a concrete plan does allow us to stay on track and be aware when we need to make a change.

CHAPTER 4 Bringing Home Your Scottish Terrier

Photo Courtesy of Linda Lukac

Pet Supplies to Have Ready

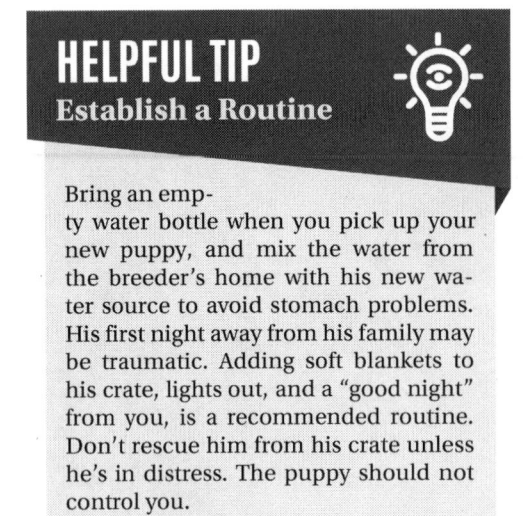

> **HELPFUL TIP**
> **Establish a Routine**
>
> Bring an empty water bottle when you pick up your new puppy, and mix the water from the breeder's home with his new water source to avoid stomach problems. His first night away from his family may be traumatic. Adding soft blankets to his crate, lights out, and a "good night" from you, is a recommended routine. Don't rescue him from his crate unless he's in distress. The puppy should not control you.

Back to my "prospective new parents" analogy; new parents don't wait until the baby is home before going out to buy diapers, a crib, or baby formula. These items are bought sometimes months in advance because the parents know the new baby will need the items and they also know they probably won't have the chance to leave the house.

Similarly, you want to ensure you have several supplies on hand before bringing home your Scottish Terrier.

You should consider purchasing a kennel or a crate for your dog. A kennel serves as a safe place for dogs not only when they're around their families but also when they are alone and must be contained to one area of the house. The kennel serves as a place to retreat from overwhelming situations, so have a kennel ready before bringing home your Scottie in case she experiences stress and needs her space.

You'll want to have puppy food, a food bowl, and a water bowl. Try to keep the same food your Scottie has been eating before you brought her home. Any bowl can be used to feed and water your dogs, but they will appreciate having bowls that are specifically theirs and that only they are allowed to eat from. Having bowls for each pet also cuts down on aggressive behavior during mealtimes, so if you have multiple pets, it's vital to purchase new pet bowls for your new Scottish Terrier.

Be sure that you bring home some new toys for the new dog to play with. While your pets may share most of their toys later, your new Scottish Terrier may be reluctant to encroach on what may be someone else's territory by playing with toys that have another animal's scent.

Cleaning supplies are a must, regardless of whether you've prepared puppy pads in your home. Your puppy may have an accident outside of the designated area, or she or another of the animals may decide to mark their territory by spraying around the house. The basic cleaning supplies you'll need are paper towels and a pet-specific cleaning solution. You can make

CHAPTER 4 Bringing Home Your Scottish Terrier

Photo Courtesy of Cathy Boyes

your own cleaning solution, but the pet-specific cleaners work to prevent stains and odors from settling into your home and help prevent marking in that area in the future.

Something you may not consider having on hand already is a collar, harness, and leash. A collar isn't 100% vital, but it does give you somewhere to place an ID tag, and most dogs actually like having a collar. It's something that smells like them, and they often get upset when their collars are removed. A collar is something that dogs may consider their property, so go ahead and buy your Scottie a collar so she can proudly display her belonging to your family. A harness and a leash are a must because your Scottish Terrier requires daily walks and should not have those walks unleashed.

The Ride Home

The ride home is likely an exciting event for both you and your new Scottish Terrier, but you may both be feeling nervousness along with that excitement. Your pup has no idea where she's going, and you have no idea how she will react to her new environment.

For safety reasons, your new puppy should not have free rein to roam around your car during the ride home. Excited dogs in a car can be a dangerous distraction. I recommend having a car harness or kennel ready before picking up your Scottie. Have someone sit in the back seat with your new pet to keep her calm, especially if the drive home is long.

The First Night Home

The first night home is likely to be stressful. Your Scottish Terrier is in a new and strange place with new and strange people. The family she's known all her short life is nowhere to be found and neither is the litter she's spent her whole life sleeping and playing with. Your Scottie puppy might be nervous around everyone and won't want to sleep alone.

It's important to make your Scottie feel secure in her new home, and if you've prepared areas for your Scottie beforehand, this step shouldn't be too difficult. Just give your Scottish Terrier all the time she needs to explore her kennel, her potty areas, her food area, and her living area in her own time. You may need to utilize snacks to convince her to enter the kennel on her own. Do not force her inside or she may never come to trust the kennel as a safe place.

Photo Courtesy of Aaron Gordon

Try to tire your Scottie out before bedtime to make the event much easier. Don't let her nap, and consider a short playtime either inside or in a fenced yard. It won't take long for your Scottie to use up a lot of energy with her small frame.

CHAPTER 4 Bringing Home Your Scottish Terrier

If you're planning to crate train, your Scottish Terrier should spend her first few nights sleeping inside of her kennel. She is likely to whine to be released, which causes another layer of stress as you worry about your new pup. With time, she will become used to being in her kennel at night, and with continued proper crate training, she will come to love being inside and will enter on her own whenever she pleases. I suggest making the kennel as comforting as possible: give your Scottie a blanket or pillow with your scent and a few toys to keep her company.

As I've already mentioned, puppies have small bladders, so you'll be waking up several times in the middle of the night to take your Scottish Terrier to her designated potty area. Nighttime may be scary for your pup at first, so be sure you've taken your Scottie to this area during daytime, and she should be able to smell where she did her business before and be comforted by the familiar scent.

Photo Courtesy of Becky Bratten

First Vet Visit/Choosing a Vet

If you haven't already chosen a veterinarian for your new pet, do so immediately. Your Scottish Terrier should visit a vet within the first few days of being in her new home to ensure her health as well as to introduce her to her new doctor. Your vet will want to see where your Scottie is health-wise so he or she can track your pup's health as she grows.

Choosing a vet shouldn't be too hard, but you do want to consider a few things. You want the veterinarian taking care of your animal companions to be trustworthy. Do online research and check reviews; pet owners aren't afraid to warn fellow pet owners from a distasteful veterinarian and will rave about an exceptional one. You can also get recommendations from any pet owners you know personally.

The vet you choose should be somewhere close to your home. If none of the vets close to your home are to your liking, you can look farther away, but you should know of somewhere close to take your Scottie if she ever has a time-sensitive accident. You don't want to waste time during an emergency trying to decide the best place to take a member of your family. Be sure you know exactly what services these veterinarian offices offer as your pet may require care that one office isn't equipped to give.

The first vet visit may be stressful for a puppy, but the more often your Scottish Terrier visits new places, the less nervous she'll be each time. The vet is no different, and it's a good idea to get your pup used to being handled as she'll likely need to be handled by both strangers and your family a lot. Scottish Terriers require a decent amount of grooming, and some of that grooming sometimes happens at the vet's office anyway.

Puppy Classes

Puppy classes are a great opportunity to bond with your new Scottish Terrier and are really important if you don't plan to do extensive training at home or aren't sure how to train a puppy properly. It's important that your puppy be vaccinated before attending classes. All dogs participating in puppy classes are supposed to have proof of vaccination, but there's always a chance that one of the dogs is sick.

Many new dog owners don't yet know how to interact with their dogs, a problem which often leads to the dog disrespecting the owner and ignoring commands. During puppy classes, an instructor can guide new owners through how to motivate their new puppy, how to teach their new puppy, and how to properly give their new puppy commands.

Of course, dogs of any age can learn new commands, but it is far easier to teach a puppy than it is to teach an adult who has settled into his ways. Puppy classes serve as an opportunity to socialize your Scottish Terrier with other dogs and with humans. According to a study from the Azabu University Graduate School of Veterinary Science, puppies who attended a six-week puppy training class were more likely to act positively toward strangers than adult dogs who attended a six-week training class and dogs who did not attend any training classes at all (adult or otherwise).

This study exemplifies the importance of early socialization, especially for the Scottish Terrier which can become aggressive toward all but a chosen few if not properly trained and socialized. Socialization is important all throughout a dog's life, but it's especially important before six months

CHAPTER 4 Bringing Home Your Scottish Terrier

of age. In fact, specialists recommend that a puppy be exposed to at least 100 people of diverse ethnicities, ages, and heights within the first month of being home. Even something as simple as eyeglasses can make a dog distrustful if she's never seen them on a person before.

Puppy classes can be both exciting and stressful, but these classes are just one hour a week for you and your puppy to learn together. When you're home, you should practice as often as possible, and you should see improvement in your puppy's behavior, socializing, and bond with you as the weeks go on.

Overall, puppy-training classes are more than just to teach your puppy a few tricks. These classes are important to teach both you and your pet the correct commands as well as to ensure your puppy is polite and well-socialized. No one wants to enter your home only to be greeted negatively by a distrustful and untrained dog.

Photo Courtesy of Caroline Reid

Cost Breakdown for the First Year

The cost of owning and caring for a Scottish Terrier varies depending on many factors. The first year is likely to be the most expensive, but that expense is more like an investment in many healthy and happy years to come.

Though it may not be the first expense you encounter when deciding to bring a new companion into your life, the adoption fee or purchase price for your Scottie is the first thing you should consider. As I mentioned earlier, adopting a Scottish Terrier may be hard since this breed is so popular, and adoption fees can range anywhere from $150 to $500, depending on how strong the breed's physical characteristics display within the pup. Of course, no pup needs to look exactly like the AKC standard, so adopted Scotties are definitely worth the adoption price.

If you're looking for stronger Scottie features or proof of a pure bloodline, you'll be paying top dollar, anywhere between $700 to $3,500. The more expensive dogs you'll find will probably come from a successful show line or may have specifically been bred to compete as show dogs, so the high price point reflects the heritage of the breed.

Vet visits are one of those expenses that will go down with time, if only because as your puppy ages, she won't need to visit the vet as much. For the first four months of a puppy's life, she should be seen at least once a month to keep her updated on vaccinations and to track her physical and behavioral development. After that age, your dog should see the vet every six months. Depending on your veterinarian as well as other factors, you could pay between $25 and $45 per visit to the vet, and that number doesn't include any tests or vaccinations the vet may need to administer.

Vaccinations and other preventive care are vital for your dog's health, and some are even required by law. From six weeks of age to three years of age, your dog should get regular vaccinations. As she grows older, she'll need fewer and fewer, but the vaccinations she receives in her first year will protect her from distemper, measles, rabies, and many other common and preventable diseases. Other preventive care can also protect your pup; flea prevention and heartworm prevention can protect your Scottie from the diseases and conditions these invasive pests cause. The first year of vaccinations can be between $0 and $300, depending on your area and access to shelter or community programs.

The cost of sterilization depends on the size and gender of a dog. The national average for sterilizing a dog is anywhere between $50 and $500. For a small-dog breed like the Scottie, that cost shouldn't reach the higher price range unless there are complications during the surgery or other considerations the veterinarian has to account for before surgery begins. Since spaying is more invasive than neutering, sterilizing female dogs will be more expensive. Of course, you may choose not to spay or neuter your dog, or you may have signed a contract with a breed preventing you from doing such. If that's the case, this won't be an expense for you.

The price of pet insurance depends on whether you're actually insuring your pet or signing up for a pet-care plan. The difference is that a care plan gives you discounts on pet supplies and vet visits while pet insurance is more about reimbursement. You may also need a specific type of insurance if you're planning to turn your Scottie into a show dog. Pet insurance

CHAPTER 4   Bringing Home Your Scottish Terrier

and care plans are really helpful because they give you peace of mind that you'll be able to pay for any unexpected medical expenses. Pet insurance averages between $10 to $100 a month.

Grooming is another optional expense, but during the first year, regardless if you groom at home or take your Scottie to a groomer, you'll need to spend money. If you're planning to groom at home, you can save yourself an average of $50 a month on grooming, but you'll need to make a one-time purchase for most of the supplies you'll need including nail trimmers or grinders, brushes, shampoos, and more. You can also choose to brush your dog's teeth at home to lower the cost of dental cleanings.

And of course, you need to take into account how much you'll be spending on toys, a collar, a harness, a leash, a crate, a travel crate, cleaning supplies, paper towels, and much more. These costs will vary depending on what you actually need and use.

EXPENSE	ESTIMATED COST
Adoption/Purchase	$150 - $3,500
Physical Exams	$100 - $180
Vaccinations/Preventive Care	$0 - $300
Heartworm Prevention/ Flea Treatment	$100 - $200
Spay/Neuter	$0 - $500
Insurance	$0 - $100
Grooming	$60 - $600
Dental Cleaning	$75 - $300
Puppy Classes	$50 - $125
Food	$250 - $700
Toys/Other Supplies	~$300

Though the first-year costs of owning a Scottish Terrier seem high, it's a price you should be prepared to pay before you actually adopt or purchase your Scottish Terrier. Remember that animals are not accessories, so when you're planning to add a new creature to your family, make sure you have the means and the desire to properly care for that creature before bringing them home.

CHAPTER 5
Being a Puppy Parent

"Scottie puppies are very strong willed even at an early age. They learn quickly they can wrap you around their little paws to get what they want."

Lainie Culton
Culton's Scottish Terriers

Standing by Your Expectations

As puppy parents, we have a lot of expectations, and that fact is true whether this is your first puppy or your fifth puppy. Our expectations can very quickly be shattered if we forget that a puppy is a living being with its own personality, and any puppy can surprise you by going against common breed personality or behavior.

Puppies share a lot of characteristics with toddlers in the early days: they can be cranky and destructive and have accidents ANY and EVERY-where if you don't watch them closely.

Depending on how old you get your puppy (12-13 weeks is what's best and required by most breeders, but you may have found yourself with a younger Scottish Terrier puppy somehow), you should expect to take one to two trips to the bathroom a night if you keep your Scottie on a training, feeding, and watering schedule.

I personally keep my dog's water outside, and he has access to it all day with restricted access at night when he's let out. Be sure that you've fully house-trained your Scottish Terrier before allowing him free access to the house.

You may have a harder time with house-training during winter. Many Scottish Terriers do just fine in cold weather as their double coat works to keep their tiny bodies insulated, but some Scotties may have recently been groomed or may not have as distinctive a long and dense Scottie coat, so that individual pup may be more susceptible to the cold. Luckily, there's a large market for doggie sweaters, and your pup would look absolutely dashing in one such sweater.

CHAPTER 5 Being a Puppy Parent

You should attempt to get your Scottie to sleep through the night. Puppies need about 18 hours of sleep a day because dogs don't go into as deep a sleep as humans. While your tiny pup will have a ton of energy after a nap, he may use that energy quickly during even a short half hour playtime.

Potty accidents and sleeping routines can be easily managed with crate training.

Kennel training is another area of dog training many puppy owners have expectations about already. Some don't want to use a kennel because they've heard bad things about how some owners use the kennel when training their pups.

Regardless of the misconception or knowledge of kennels and crates one may have, the fact is that with proper crate training, your pup will learn to love his crate because he understands it is a safe place for him to be not only when he wants to be inside but also when you have to leave him home alone.

Dogs have many of the same instincts that they've had since before they were our devoted best friends, and the long-proven method of communicating and training our pups involves focusing on rewarding the positive behaviors our animal companions display.

Photo Courtesy of Verna Bardsley

How to Crate Train

While crate training your Scottie, you should work with your Scottie's natural instinct to feel sheltered inside of a den-like structure. Your Scottish Terrier's instincts make him want to hunker down to wait out a storm or just to preserve warmth or feel safe while he naps. A crate provides this sense of safety, and with a well-placed blanket and heat-source, you can spoil your Scottie silly with his own warm space in your family's home. Remember, Scottish Terriers enjoy having their own space. These dogs are independent, and although they love being with their pack, these warriors don't want to be lap dogs.

To introduce your Scottish Terrier to his crate, slowly let him explore the open space in his own time. About three months into your puppy's life is vital for his confidence as this is the point in time when he is most easily imprinted with long-lasting fears.

If you force your Scottie into his crate, especially if you leave him there and he eliminates there because he couldn't hold his bladder long, he may never become comfortable with the crate.

If you leave fun things in your Scottie's open crate, he'll enter and get comfortable when he feels like it. A shirt with your scent on it, an old pillow, or an enticing squeaky toy is usually enough to entice a puppy to settle into a space, but you can use treats and regular meals to convince your Scottish Terrier puppy that his crate is a safe place just for him to enjoy life.

Start your crate training as early as possible. The sooner your pup learns the status quo, the sooner he can get to be a happy watchdog patrolling his territory or keeping your garden free from annoying pests or keeping you company as you work from home. Whatever role your Scottish Terrier fills in your life, remember that he deserves a space to call his own within the family home, and without a crate, which is basically a tiny room, a dog's space in the home can become ambiguous.

You can set your Scottish Terrier's crate up in any area close to where the family spends most of its time. This area may change with the seasons as some rooms may be better for some seasons. In the main living area, your animals may share a cozy rug next to a cozy chair with your Scottie's crate behind the chair. In the back of the house, you may want to place his kennel in a corner of the hall between all of the bedrooms or have a corner for him in a bedroom. Wherever you place your dog's crate depends on your family's available space.

Scotties are small dogs, but crates can take up more space than the pups they house. Remember that you may need to quickly command your

CHAPTER 5 Being a Puppy Parent

Scottish Terrier to enter his crate to get him safely out of your way. You want the entrance and door to be accessible and unblocked.

In fact, your Scottie's crate should be left open so he may enter as he pleases. Your dog's crate should make him feel safe and secure. If there are children in the home, your dog may need to enter his crate to get away from them. If you have guests or visitors to your home, your dog may choose to spend his time in his crate rather than anywhere else in the house.

Remember that dog training is all about exposing your dog to situations and associating certain feelings with that situation. If you crate your dog only when you're leaving the home, he will associate his crate with anxious feelings. Even though the crate is supposed to be a place your dog can freely enter and exit, there are times when you're home that you should crate your Scottish Terrier.

When you're cleaning or cooking and need your pup to be out of the way, crate him! He'll be fine for half an hour, especially if his crate is somewhere from which he can observe you. Make sure he has toys to occupy himself, and eventually, you may not need to close his crate door to get him to stay inside when directed.

Photo Courtesy of Freya Juniper-Nine

Bedtime

Bedtime is important for puppies since they need to gather their energy for all the growing they'll be doing within the first year of life. Puppies need between 15 and 20 hours of sleep a day since they don't sleep as long or as deeply in one sitting as humans do.

Setting and following a schedule for your puppy's sleep can form a stable outline that frames his day-to-day life and fits your own schedule as much as you need it to.

Photo Courtesy of Monique Dearlove

Your puppy will nap periodically throughout the day from between 30 minutes to an hour at a time, usually after walks or playtime.

Your puppy should know what areas of the house he's allowed to sleep in, and he should have several options for comfortable and quiet sleeping. If you need to, you can guide him to the specific spot you want him to sleep when he starts to get drowsy and seems as if he needs a nap.

At night, you'll be glad that you've set up a sleep routine as your puppy will become used to sleeping throughout the night. Dogs thrive on routine, and starting early with a sleep routine will keep your nights peaceful for years to come.

Keep your Scottie's sleeping area quiet and dimmed when it's bedtime. If your dog sleeps in an area with a lot of light shining onto his sleeping area, utilize blankets to cover his crate and keep the light out.

Avoid feeding and watering your pup 30-60 minutes before bed. Consider a walk before bedtime to wear out your Scottish Terrier puppy. Be prepared to take at least one potty trip in the middle of the night for the first months. As your puppy grows, so will his ability to hold his bladder and sleep through the night.

CHAPTER 5   Being a Puppy Parent

Chewing

Chewing and biting go hand in hand with dogs because it's one of the only ways they have to communicate with us or to interact with the world. Chewing up your shoes may be a sign that your Scottie is displeased when you leave for work. Biting when you spend too much time petting him may be a sign he's ready for his own time. Either way, chewing and biting can be terrible habits to deal with because they're both destructive and dangerous.

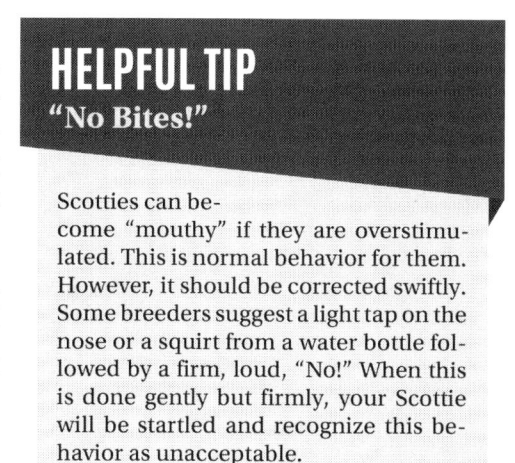

> **HELPFUL TIP**
> **"No Bites!"**
>
> Scotties can become "mouthy" if they are overstimulated. This is normal behavior for them. However, it should be corrected swiftly. Some breeders suggest a light tap on the nose or a squirt from a water bottle followed by a firm, loud, "No!" When this is done gently but firmly, your Scottie will be startled and recognize this behavior as unacceptable.

Your Scottie may nip, chew, or bite for many reasons. When pups are with their mothers and littermates, nipping is usually how they all communicate with each other and get each other's attention. They may nip your ankles to get your attention, but you aren't one of their littermates, and this behavior can be annoying.

If your Scottie gets into the habit of biting to warn you or communicate some displeasure, he may become a danger to others he doesn't care about as much as you; his bite may not be as mild in that case, and there are a range of unpleasant punishments your Scottie could incur depending on the situation.

To control biting, nipping, and chewing, you need to show your pup that his behavior is unwanted and unacceptable. When your Scottie nips you or your clothing to get your attention, give him the no command and ignore him. The same is true if the biting happens during playtime; even though your Scottish Terrier may be having fun, he needs to learn that chewing on humans is inappropriate.

Additionally, you can redirect the chewing and biting to appropriate toys. Puppies go through a teething stage during which they'll want to chew on anything to relieve their itchy gums, so provide teething rings and any other items your dog has permission to chew on. Doing so can protect your pillows and shoes.

You may need to use a spray bottle full of water to dissuade chewing while repeating the no or no biting command. Loud noises also help to get your dog's attention and deter bad habits. Crating can also help control chewing during times when your Scottie is unattended.

Growling and Barking

Growling and barking are not always signs of aggression. Oftentimes, these behaviors are signs that your puppy is comfortable in his home or enjoying himself. Again, there are few ways for dogs to communicate with humans, and when your Scottish Terrier is especially happy during playtime, he may bark excessively or growl to show pleasure. Your Scottie will expressive himself in several ways.

Your Scottish Terrier may growl or bark at animals or other passersby in the house, and this behavior is normal for this territorial breed. He may be warning someone off from coming closer, or he may merely be curious about the strange vehicles he watches pass by.

Aggressive growling with Scotties can occur when your dog is annoyed by another dog or by a human. The growl is a warning, and Scottish Terriers aren't afraid to follow that fair warning up with a sharp lesson.

Frustrated growls are important to understand and pay attention to; this type of growling may sound like an accusation because it's your dog's way of saying "you've ignored me/my needs/my desires." Growling and barking can also convey that your Scottie wants to be left alone, is injured, is afraid, wants to fight, or is already on the verge of starting a fight.

When you want to control your Scottie's barking, the quiet command is the way to go. Train your Scottie to be quiet when you command by rewarding him the moment he stops barking after giving him the quiet command. With a few well-timed treats, your Scottish Terrier can come to learn when you need his silence.

As you spend more time with your Scottish Terrier, you'll come to recognize what his different growls and barks mean, and it's important for the humans living and interacting with your Scottish Terrier to understand what his growling and barking mean.

Don't forget that the sounds dogs make are much less important than their body language. You can tell a lot about what a dog wants from the noises he makes, but his body language will reveal his mood and maybe even his next move.

CHAPTER 5   Being a Puppy Parent

Digging

It's just a fact of life that Terriers like to dig, so you need to be prepared for your Scottish Terrier puppy to dig. This breed was cultivated to hunt vermin and manage pests hiding in the mountains and on farms in the rocky Scotland Highlands.

Your own Scottish Terrier may dig for any number of reasons, from being bored to wanting to chase a cat to preferring to be on your neighbor's side of the fence. Whatever the situation, you need to direct your Scottie's urge to dig to appropriate places and dissuade him from digging in inappropriate places.

Provide your Scottish Terrier with a place of his own where the dirt can easily be dug up. He'll soon learn that your flowerbeds are not a good place for him to do his digging. Additionally, you may consider investing in a fence that extends farther beneath the ground or surround the inside border of your fence with cinder blocks.

You may also choose to entertain your Scottish Terrier in another way, preventing him from wanting to dig in the first place. Stimulation is important for dogs, and an empty, toy-less yard presents your dog with few options for fun. Curb the desire to dig by providing more stimulation for your dog in his outside area.

Running Away

If you haven't considered microchipping, having a Scottish Terrier may change your mind. Scotties are smart and can be determined when attempting to escape confinement.

If your yard isn't properly fenced off and you have a lot of patio furniture near gates, your Scottish Terrier can easily escape your yard. A Scottish Terrier may run away to chase another animal, out of fear, or just because it feels like patrolling an area.

When you're out in public, your Scottie must always be leashed. The breed's instinct to chase is strong, and while a well-trained Scottish Terrier can overcome his instincts and stay close to you as trained, it's better to be safe than sorry with the safety of your Scottie.

To prevent your Scottish Terrier from running away, make sure your yard is secured and make sure your Scottie has entertainment to distract him from anything outside of your yard. Your Scottie won't be tempted to run away if he has nothing to run away to, so consider a privacy fence or bushes that block your dog's view and access to your neighborhood.

Separation Anxiety

Photo Courtesy of Michelle Lynch

Dogs of various breeds suffer from separation anxiety when their owners must leave them alone. Dogs are pack animals, so you should expect your Scottie to display separation anxiety at some point in his life, and owners sometimes make matters worse by leaving their dogs alone in their crates for too long.

Separation anxiety can lead to destructive behavior that can leave your home in shambles, both you and your dog emotionally upset, and can potentially leave your dog physically injured if he gets worked up enough to avoid injuries to himself in an attempt to escape or find you. Separation anxiety can exacerbate or even be the cause of many common behavioral problems dog owners report.

To help relieve separation anxiety, slowly begin training your Scottish Terrier to be along for small stretches of time. You can do this simply by leaving your dog to an activity then going to a different room in your house. Return to your dog periodically, especially to check for and correct any misbehaviors.

The most important thing is not to make your leaving or arriving something more than it is. You shouldn't greet your dog in an excited manner when you arrive home, and you shouldn't drag out leaving home in the morning.

Separation anxiety is something that typically builds within a dog, so the longer he knows you are leaving, the more time he'll be making himself sick so that by the time you do leave, he's already at the point of acting out in fear.

Leaving Your Dog Home Alone

Leaving your Scottish Terrier home alone may be unavoidable if you have a job or any responsibilities outside of the home. Once your Scottie is fully house-trained, he can be left alone for as long as he can hold his bladder and as long as he has access to food, water, and toys.

You'll want to ensure your house is fully dog-proofed or consider crating for the duration of your absence. Scotties don't generally enjoy being left alone despite their independence, so someone should check on your Scottie about every four hours if you need to regularly leave him home alone. It's dangerous to leave your Scottie unattended for longer than four hours, and some trainers advise against leaving this breed alone outside because of escape attempts.

Dog music is becoming more and more popular, so if you do need to leave your pup alone, you can leave soothing separation anxiety music playing to help relieve some of your dog's stress, or you can hire a dog walker to stop by in the middle of your workday to make sure your Scottish Terrier has his needs attended to while you're away.

CHAPTER 6
House-Training

Different Options for Potty Training

Depending on your housing needs, the option you choose for house-training may be as simple as installing a doggy door out to your backyard or as complex as having a portable potty grass patch because you live on the top floor of your apartment when your puppy's bladder is the most active it'll ever be. You may decide to set up a pet potty area on a patio or in a specific corner of your yard or in your laundry room for the winter.

Any of these options are valid if they fit your lifestyle, and your Scottish Terrier can be house-trained with any of these potty-training methods.

You should also consider a schedule for walks or going out to pee. In the early days, your Scottie will pee about every hour, and after, it'll be as long as he can hold it and during regular times after he's eaten and probably during walks. Your Scottish Terrier needs a certain amount of exercise every day, so this bathroom schedule can merely be built into that schedule.

Monitoring when your pup drinks and eats can help you predict when you should take your Scottish Terrier for a walk. Ten to 60 minutes after eating or drinking is a good estimate to work with. If you work from home, you could even plan your own breaks around your Scottie's bathroom schedule.

Choosing when and where your Scottie should relieve herself is just the first step to successful house-training, and as the weeks turn into months, you'll want assurance that your Scottish Terrier truly understands where she is and isn't allowed to relieve herself.

> **HELPFUL TIP**
> **Pick a Spot**
>
> Picking a spot outside where you want your dog to relieve himself is essential. He should be taken outside upon removal from his crate in the morning, thirty minutes after meals, and before bedtime. Consistently using a signal word such as "potty" will help your dog understand what is expected of him. Praise him when he is successful, but do not give food treats for expected toileting behavior.

CHAPTER 6 House-Training

The First Few Weeks

From the moment your Scottish Terrier comes home, you should be training her. One of the first places in her new home your Scottie should spend time is her bathroom area.

Whether inside or out, there should be one approved area for your dog to relieve herself so she doesn't get confused about where to pee and start leaving damp surprises on every carpet in the house.

Hang around with your Scottie in this approved area until she's done her business. Don't speak until she's about to relieve herself, and then speak only to give her the command to "potty."

Photo Courtesy of Claudia Granados

Wait for your pup to relieve both her bladder and her bowels so she knows that both belong in the same area. Reward her with praise and attention for relieving herself in an approved area. In general, just pay attention to your puppy as well as her feeding schedule, and you should be able to predict when she'll need to go out.

Every morning when your puppy wakes up, take her to her bathroom area and command her to "potty" or "get busy" or whatever command you decide to use for your Scottie. You don't want your Scottish Terrier to merely be used to relieving herself in the approved place; she should know that the approved place is the ONLY place she should relieve herself. Additionally, teaching your Scottie a command she recognizes to relieve herself can put her at ease if she ever needs to use the bathroom in an unfamiliar place.

Consistency is key with dogs. Routine and familiarity will put a dog at ease. When you set boundaries for your Scottish Terrier, she feels safe knowing what to expect because she'll follow your lead and your rules as long as you teach her kindly and patiently.

Rewarding Positive Behavior

Rewarding positive behaviors works best when we reward the behaviors we want our pets to display and ignore the ones we don't like. There ARE times when you'll need to make it clear to your pet that her behavior is unacceptable or that a certain area is certainly off limits, but in general, our dogs will continue to act out whatever behaviors we reward them for.

No one likes only hearing when they are wrong or when they've done something bad. Pet parents who use the "come here" command only when reprimanding their dogs soon find that their pups won't "come here" at all because they know they'll be in trouble as soon as Mom or Dad catches them.

Photo Courtesy of Emily Ashworth

Dogs respond well to positive reinforcement and clear boundaries, and successfully training your Scottish Terrier is all about clearly communicating to your pup when she's done something correctly.

The simplest way to express that your Scottie has done something right is by saying "good girl." Pair the praise with a treat, and she will soon learn that being a good girl has its benefits.

Of course, you can mix and match many different rewards when training your Scottish Terrier. Depending on the level of difficulty and the number of commands your Scottie has learned, she may earn anything from a few soft chews to some crunchy homemade peanut butter bites.

You may choose to use toys instead of treats altogether, but I prefer a mix of treats and toys as rewards. The more complex the command, the more complex the treat. Your pup's favorite treats or toys should, of course, be the highest reward to achieve, so plan training accordingly so your pup doesn't come to expect a reward for following the simplest of commands.

CHAPTER 6 House-Training

Crate Training for House-Training Use

Your Scottish Terrier puppy won't be able to hold her bladder for longer than an hour at a time, so smart planning is needed to keep her on track to successful house-training. Preventing indoor accidents and teaching your Scottie where and when to empty her bladder can protect you and your precious floor from many unpleasant surprises and frequent cleanings.

Dogs will avoid going to the bathroom in their living areas, so the smartest way to house-train your Scottish Terrier is to make her feel at home in every area of your home so she won't even want to soil the living area.

Crate training provides a stable foundation for helping your Scottie feel at home. The crate you choose for your Scottish Terrier should be proportioned to her size. I recommend anything between 24-inches and 30-inches, depending on your specific dog.

This crate should be big enough for your Scottie to walk around in a circle and stretch out in comfortably. Anything bigger and your dog may relieve herself in a corner far enough away from her sleeping area, setting back her house-training. If you have a crate bigger than that because you expect your pup to grow some, you can buy or make a crate divider to make the crate fit your needs.

Don't be afraid to move your puppy's crate around to different areas of the house and leave it open for her to enter and explore in her own time. Leave toys and treats in those areas, and she'll keep her eliminations in the designated place they belong.

Your puppy will need to go to the bathroom every morning after waking up or after eating, so you'll have control over her bathroom schedule from the moment she leaves her crate in the morning, ready to take on the day.

Early on in this training you may want to carry your puppy to the designated bathroom spot so she doesn't just pee the moment

Photo Courtesy of Catherine Moats

she steps from her crate, but as your puppy gains confidence in your training, she should be trusted to walk herself to go outside or to her puppy pads after waking up.

After meals is another time during which you can expect your Scottish Terrier puppy to relieve herself. Five to sixty minutes is the typical wait for a puppy to need to go out, so don't take your eye off her during the early days of training or else you'll be scrubbing stains out of your carpet.

Exercise can stimulate your Scottie's need to relieve herself, so walks in the morning and before bed can prepare both you and your animal companion for the day as well as the night. Don't forget to praise your Scottish Terrier for responsibly going to the bathroom where she's supposed to. Consider using a clicker device or a small bell to indicate to your Scottie when she's being praised, and again, back up that praise with treats and toys on occasion, and some physical affection in the form of pets and belly rubs wouldn't hurt either.

Photo Courtesy of Linda Lukac

CHAPTER 6 House-Training

Playpens and Doggy Doors

A playpen can offer another area for your Scottish Terrier to call her own. With all of her toys in one area, the rest of your home can stay tidy, and a well-placed playpen can ensure that your Scottish Terrier feels secure while you're away in another room. The Scottie is independent enough to be near you and won't feel the need to follow you through every room in the house.

You can add the playpen to your house-training routine as your Scottish Terrier will want to avoid getting waste on her toys, and you can also use the playpen to keep your Scottie from other others of the home such as a cat's litter area or the kitchen during mealtimes.

Doggy doors are an option for older and more independent dogs who are fully house-trained and can be trusted to relieve themselves in the appropriate areas. Additionally, a doggy door can help relieve stress for anxious dogs by giving them the ability to relieve themselves as needed and to get more stimulation by changing their environments. Just ensure that the area the doggy door lets out to is fully secured against escape either over or under the border of your property.

CHAPTER 7
Socializing with People and Animals

"Scottish Terriers are very aloof by nature. To develop a very friendly outgoing Scottie, socialize them a lot. Take them to the coffee shop, to the hardware store; go on walks with friends that have dogs. A friendly Scottie is a great ambassador of the breed."

Lainie Culton
Culton's Scottish Terriers

Importance of Good Socialization

Anyone who has had the pleasure of having an animal companion knows that proper socialization contributes greatly to the mental health, temperament, and long-term behavior of a growing creature.

When you bring home your Scottish Terrier puppy for the first time, realize that he hasn't been away from his litter or the place he was born for longer than it takes to make a visit to the vet and return home. He has been socialized as a dog with his litter, but now he must be socialized and properly introduced to his new life with his human companions.

The term *socialization* in the context of dog training is all about introducing your dog to new and diverse situations, an action which both helps to ensure proper socialization for your Scottish Terrier and contributes to his lifelong happiness.

Socialization concerns how your puppy reacts to people and places and is all about how you've interacted with your Scottie and how you've taught him to react through your own actions. A properly socialized dog should not fear or flinch away from new humans. In the very early days of your dog's life, every interaction he has can contribute to how he acts and reacts for the rest of his life.

A properly socialized dog also shouldn't be overly aggressive toward humans. This age in a puppy's life is a good time to perhaps train your

CHAPTER 7   Socializing with People and Animals

Scottie not to bark when your visitors come over. Some owners like to train their pups to carry a toy or pillow to present to guests when they arrive so their dogs never have the opportunity to bark.

How you react to your pup and interact with him contributes greatly to his personality. Positive reinforcement and plenty of encouragement will keep your Scottish Terrier from being too fearful or distrustful of those who don't belong to the household.

> **HELPFUL TIP**
> **Handle with Loving Care**
>
> Owners should establish dominance over their new dog by picking him up, holding him close to their face, and staring into his eyes. Don't look away first! When your puppy looks away, he will know that you are the pack leader. Then hold him close and praise him. On the floor, roll your dog onto his side and pin him down briefly and gently with care. This will let him know who is the boss, and ensure proper socialization.

Conversely, how you respond to your puppy's reactions will affect how he reacts in the future. Have patience understanding and communicating with your Scottish Terrier, and reward his positive behaviors with positive reinforcement.

Lack of socialization might be your main worry, but keep in mind that overexposing your Scottish Terrier to your presence can lead to an over-reliance on you for a sense of safety. If you allow your Scottish Terrier to follow you to places such as the bathroom or out to get the mail, he may be unable to adjust without your presence, even if you're just in another room in your home.

The number of diverse individuals (dog, human, or otherwise) your Scottie interacts with is another aspect of proper socialization on which to focus. In general, dogs can become fearful or aggressive for any reason from a negative experience to fear of the unknown from lack of exposure.

Your Scottish Terrier will be watchful of anyone and anything that he has little to no experience with, so expose your Scottie to dogs of different breeds and sizes as well as humans of different sexes, ethnicities, and styles (accessories such as glasses, hats, and umbrellas can startle the uninitiated pup).

Photo Courtesy of Ann Marie French

Behavior Around Other Dogs

Even though Scottish Terriers aren't known to be friendly with other dogs, your individual method of socializing your pup may result in a loving and friendly Scottish Terrier who has no problem making and maintaining doggy friendships.

Teach your puppy how and when to be calm around other dogs whose owners may have invested varying amounts of attention and training toward the betterment of their dog's temperament.

A puppy class or a one-on-one puppy playdate is a good way to introduce your Scottish Terrier to other dogs for the first time or to test your Scottish Terrier's behavior around other dogs before less structured interactions. After a few successful playdates, consider introducing your Scottie to the dog park where he can be exposed to many different dogs as well as their owners. At a dog park, anyone can be a playmate.

You may discover how feisty these dogs can be if your Scottie displays some of the antisocial characteristics common to the breed. Many Scottish Terriers show no fear toward dogs who are bigger than they are, and some may be quick to start fights without warning.

Some signs of aggression to watch for include nipping and biting, growling and snarling, baring teeth, lunging forward, becoming rigid, or any other action that indicates an impending attack. Remember, early socialization and training can reduce and prevent aggressive behaviors.

CHAPTER 7   Socializing with People and Animals

Ways to Socialize Your Dog with Other Pets

"Introduce your Scottie puppy to other pets gradually. Socialize him or her with other dogs only once he or she has had all the necessary vaccinations."

Jane Herron
Herron's Sandhills Scotties

If you have other animals who aren't dogs, you should introduce your Scottish Terrier to them as early as possible so he can become used to them. It may simply be dangerous to own an older, unsocialized Scottish Terrier if you already have other animals that may trigger the dog's prey instinct. Many non-canine pets are small and quick, quite like the farm vermin the ancestors of the Scottie hunted on a daily basis.

Without intervention from a human to ensure a low-tension introduction, animals such as dogs and cats will fight and chase and hurt each other. If you have non-canine animals, friends with non-canine animals, or plans to own non-canine animals, it's best to socialize your Scottie with as many different animals as you can.

Cats are the most likely non-canine animal your dog will meet. A good way to socialize your Scottish Terrier with cats is to start introductions slowly with both animals in separate rooms. Let them smell each other through the door. Watch for growls from your Scottie and from the cat.

When you're ready for face-to-face introductions, leash your pup, and keep him in one area without letting him roam. Consider leaving the cat in a carrier. If your Scottish Terrier is especially excited and attempting to get to the cat, gently but firmly keep him seated or in a lying position (NOT on his back).

You can feed one or both animals during this time to distract them from each other as well as to get them used to each other. This process helps to desensitize your dog to the presence of the cat by making the fact that there is a cat around nothing special.

Once your Scottie has calmed enough not to pull against the leash in an attempt to get to the cat, you can start rewarding him for certain actions he performs. Start with rewarding him for acknowledging the cat's presence by successfully looking away when prompted. Raise the actions and the reward over the next few days and weeks until both animals have become desensitized to each other's presence.

Photo Courtesy of Sarah Cole

CHAPTER 7 Socializing with People and Animals

Properly Greeting New People

How you introduce your Scottish Terrier to new people depends on his previous behavior with you and your family. In general, introductions made with a fully leashed dog are safe, but if your Scottie is particularly excitable, you may decide to confine him to a room and introduce him to new people scent-first through the door.

When it's time to meet face-to-face, have the strange new human choose a treat to give your Scottie, but make sure this human knows to let your dog make the first move to approach to avoid rewarding shyness or fearfulness.

Don't let your Scottish Terrier have the treat if he is timid or standoffish with a new human, but give him plenty of positive reinforcement once he does let himself be enticed with treats and the promise of a belly rub.

Scottish Terriers and Children

Just as in the case of other dogs and animals, a Scottish Terrier who has gone too long unsocialized may not be the best fit for a household with children, but Scotties can be socialized with children as easily as with anyone else as long as the children are respectful.

Let your child approach your Scottish Terrier from the side during the first introduction, and allow him to sniff the child while giving your Scottie plenty of space to move away if he feels uncomfortable.

Keep a watchful eye on small children, and never leave your Scottie alone with your new dog until you've observed their interactions. A Scottish Terrier may become snappish toward children who poke and prod, so it's up to the adults to keep everyone safe. Dogs enjoy a gentle touch, which a well-guided child can surely provide.

Photo Courtesy of Kayley Wilson

CHAPTER 8
Scottish Terriers and Your Other Pets

Pack Mentality

In a wild dog or wolf pack, a dam, a sire, and offspring from the last three of the alpha couple's litters live together. To dogs, a pack is a family as well as a social hierarchy, and a dog's behavior reflects her place in that social hierarchy. The pack-minded nature of dogs allows them to get along easily with animals of other species.

A typical pack for a dog now is one that involves humans and dogs and sometimes other animals, and at the center of such a pack should be a capable and responsible adult human, able to properly manage the different interactions between all the members of the pack.

Make it clear to your Scottish Terrier that any human children in your household are higher up in the pack hierarchy. This task is best completed by ensuring your children understand how to give your Scottie commands and that your Scottie actually follows those commands when given. Scottish Terriers respond to strong and clear leadership, and it's easy to be loving while also having a strong leading hand.

Photo Courtesy of Yvonne Maddocks

CHAPTER 8   Scottish Terriers and Your Other Pets

Photo Courtesy of Aaron Gordon

Introducing Your New Puppy to the Other Pack Members

You should already be established as the leader of your pack, and how you train and treat your Scottish Terrier from the moment she arrives home shows her both your place and her place in the pack, but for every other non-human member, decisions about the social hierarchy shouldn't involve you despite the fact that you are the leader.

Besides stopping and preventing aggressive behavior, you should let your animals socialize with each other and figure each other out in their own time. You should step in only to discipline a member of the pack who is breaking one of the rules you've set.

In a blended pack, the "alpha dog" may change day-to-day or as circumstances change. For instance, your dogs may all adhere to the leadership of one dog, but all your animals may cower before your cat's mighty leadership.

Conflicts may arise during any part of the pack's day and sometimes for a seemingly mundane reason. Either way, as long as your animals aren't physically harming each other, they can manage themselves, and your job is just to ensure everyone knows and follows the rules.

Tracey SQUAIRE | The Complete Guide to Scottish Terriers

*Photo Courtesy of
Joanne Sturgess*

Raising Multiple Puppies from the Same Litter

Experts suggest that you shouldn't raise puppies from the same litter together because they may be harder to train and may form an overattachment to each other that isolates humans from the relationship. While there are barriers to happily raising two puppies at the same time, the task is possible with some planning.

With Scottish Terrier puppies, it's best that there are at least two adults within your household who can take care of these puppies. Puppies from the same litter or who are being raised together should be trained both together and separately and have separate playtimes. You may consider hiring a private trainer for one or more of your puppies if you live alone.

> **HELPFUL TIP**
> **Scrappy Scotties**
>
> Scottish Terriers are not low-energy dogs. They can be standoffish with strangers, and downright aggressive with other dogs. Your strong-willed Scottie can be an intimidating watchdog, so socialize him early and often. Remember, your terrier has been bred to chase and seize small animals. Keep him on a leash whenever he is outside of the home.

Puppies raised together often form a strong bond, but they are also prone to fighting a lot since they tend to spend a good deal of time together. If you're considering two puppies so they have company while you're away, keep in mind that those puppies aren't guaranteed to like each other just because they were raised together.

Fighting/Bad Behavior

Even dogs who have lived together for some time may start fighting with each other if certain resources like food, resting places, or family attention get distributed unequally or if one dog decides to take all the resources for himself. Dogs of the same gender may fight more than those of differing genders.

If your dogs do begin fighting, your own safety needs to be uppermost in mind when stopping the fight. Keep your body and your limbs away from the dogs as even the most loyal dog will instinctively turn to bite or scratch in the middle of a fight without considering who they're attacking. Use water

Photo Courtesy of Nichola Hennessey

CHAPTER 8   Scottish Terriers and Your Other Pets

from a hose or from a spray bottle to interrupt a fight, or grab a broomstick or chair to place between the battling dogs.

Scottish Terriers may bark excessively if there's a lot of traffic around the home. A Scottie may be prone to fighting with the other animals in the neighborhood or even with the animals in your household.

If ever your dog's behavior gets to the point that your training at home isn't helping, you should seek a professional dog behaviorist or dog trainer. Bad behavior is unlikely to go away on its own, and you risk injury to your dog, another animal, or yourself by ignoring bad behavior.

Spaying and neutering can reduce aggression in dogs and prevent some of the urges that instigate dog fights, but sometimes the only option if your pets can't get along is to rehome one or both of the animals.

Look within your community for rehoming options, and consider options like no-kill shelters or foster homes. Many shelters around America are specific to the Scottish Terrier breed and will be happy to help if you need to rehome your Scottie. A breeder may accept the return of a puppy purchased from their litter.

CHAPTER 9
Physical and Mental Exercise

"Scottie's do well in apartments with a daily walk, but their love for exercise can vary. I've had some that will go on 8-10 mile hikes, while the other is happier curled up in the bottom of stroller sleeping."

Lainie Culton
Culton's Scottish Terriers

Exercise Requirements

Like anything in life, the only way to make sure your dog has daily exercise is to make his daily exercise part of your daily routine. Even 30 minutes of walking is hard to fit into a busy day if you haven't already made it a priority. When you choose to accept an animal into your life, monetary resources aren't the only thing you're sacrificing to enjoy the company of your Scottish Terrier.

Scottish Terriers require daily mental and physical stimulation, and both are vital to the growth and development of your dog. Dogs without sufficient exercise are at higher risk for obesity, frustration, and behavioral problems. Without an outlet to release his natural energy, your dog will either use that energy however he can within your home or he will lose that energy as his body becomes used to a soft, too-easy life.

Scottish Terriers are small dogs, so the moment you notice your dog's small frame expanding, visit your veterinarian to rule out health problems, then set your pup on an exercise schedules. Withdrawn behavior can result from lack of sufficient mental and physical stimulation, so your veterinarian may diagnose your Scottie with depression and recommend treatment.

Scottish Terriers have short legs, but these dogs were bred to hunt and fight; they have plenty of energy, and although a daily half hour walk is sufficient to meet the exercise requirements for these pups (along with regular play), Scotties do love long walks at times, and your Scottish Terrier may have come from a line that has even recently been competing in agility shows.

CHAPTER 9 Physical and Mental Exercise

Different Types of Exercise to Try

If you're unsure where to start with exercising your Scottish Terrier, simply visit your veterinarian for a health checkup, and she can recommend an exercise routine based on your dog's breed, age, and health.

There are as many ways to exercise your dog as you're willing to invest your time in. If your schedule is busy, try planning your own exercise time during your dog's exercise time. Ensuring your Scottish Terrier is properly exercised can help you to ensure the same for yourself.

Here's the basic routine I aim to complete with my Beagle every day. Some days we do more than listed, and some days we do less. It depends on the weather and our energy level, but we try to do as much as we can, as should you and your Scottish Terrier. Exercise is important for your and your dog's long-term health, so make it a priority in your life.

Photo Courtesy of Aaron Gordon

Photo Courtesy of
Verna Bardsley

CHAPTER 9   Physical and Mental Exercise

7:15 AM — 15-30 minute walk:	Wake up and prepare yourselves for the day. Take doggy bags, especially if your Scottie has had his breakfast already.
9:00 AM — 10-15 minute backyard play	Between the first walk and now, free play is acceptable. This scheduled time is specifically for me to socialize my dog. We do dancing and agility exercises sometimes, but fetch is a typical game of ours.
12:30 PM — 20-40 minute walk	An after-lunch walk for you and perhaps for your pup if you've scheduled his meals as such. Length of walk time depends on weather and energy. Some days are hotter than others and, therefore, more draining.
3:30 PM — 15-25 minute backyard play	This longer session is meant to allow us to get as much sun as possible before the later part of the day. Arthur and I may lounge on a blanket with our cats after playtime.
6:30 PM — Feeding + 15-30 minute backyard play	The sun sometimes doesn't set until 8:00 p.m. during a Florida summer, but I like to keep a consistent routine. It's the last outside playtime before bed, so make it count! While there may be trips outside after this time, this is the last of our outside time.

Walking and backyard play are just the tip of the iceberg. A brisk daily walk or game of fetch can benefit both you and your pup, but you can also implement dancing, doggy yoga, or team agility exercises into your daily routine. Agility exercises specifically are great for your dog's mental and physical health, so consider investing in agility equipment for your Scottie.

You can make your own agility course in your backyard and set your own rules for how agility games are won. You can also place your pup in an agility group or class where he can interact with and learn from other agility dogs. To avoid injury, spend time warming up before beginning any exercise with your dog.

Tracey SQUAIRE | The Complete Guide to Scottish Terriers

Photo Courtesy of Dadan Chavis

CHAPTER 9   Physical and Mental Exercise

Importance of Mental Exercise

Even after meeting your Scottie's basic physical needs, you should allot part of your daily life to ensuring your animal companion doesn't spend all his time bored and lounging in front of a window all day, moving only to bark at the occasional passerby. Unfortunately, many dogs spend every day in this manner with minimal physical or mental stimulation.

Mental stimulation is equally as important as physical stimulation, if not more so. Without proper mental stimulation, your dog may not even feel the need to partake in physical stimulation. No matter the age of your Scottish Terrier, you should spend time every day stimulating your dog's mind.

> **HELPFUL TIP**
> **Exercise**
>
> Because of his short legs and stout body, your Scottish Terrier will need a long walk or mild run daily. He will not be a running companion. Allow your Scottie to sniff and explore outdoors while he is safely on a leash. Watch closely, as your Scottie may want to run off in search of small critters. Dog parks are not recommended for this breed.

Mental stimulation alleviates the effects of boredom which can include withdrawn behavior, destructive behavior, anxious behavior, or hyperactive behavior. Additionally, mental stimulation is important for your dog's happiness. This necessary stimulation must come from the members of your pack either directly or through activities your Scottie is allowed to participate in.

Mental exercise can be achieved either during physical exercise or in its own separate time. Going down new paths when walking or showing your pup a new way to get to a familiar location is one way you can mentally stimulate your Scottish terrier. Creating or purchase dog puzzles is another way to provide mental stimulation.

A smell-based scavenger hunt is always fun and is both mentally and physically stimulating. Your dog's nose is way stronger than yours, and your Scottie will love digging through preapproved areas of your yard to find the special toy or treat you've left for him. This exercise is also a good way to teach your pup the appropriate digging places in your yard.

Photo Courtesy of Ann Marie French

Tips for Keeping Your Scottish Terrier Occupied

You can't always be around to stimulate your Scottish Terrier, and neither should you provide all of his stimulation. Your Scottish Terrier is already independent, and that independence will help him to keep himself entertained when you are otherwise engaged.

There are so many options on the market for occupying your dog such as mats in which you can hide snacks for your Scottie to dig out of hiding or toys that make sounds that will stimulate your dog's auditory senses or even videos designed to keep your dog relaxed and entertained.

If I'm home with my Beagle, I prefer not to spend the whole day in the same room with him because we both become attached. I set up a play area for him in another room with interactive toys such as balls that move on their own to convince dogs to play. I also put a doggy TV YouTube video on in the background to set the tone for playtime.

Consider cultivating a specific playtime experience for your Scottish Terrier. An inside scavenger hunt can keep him occupied for a good while if the treasures he finds are worth the work of tracking. A pile of safe-for-play pillows or blankets make a good hiding spot for several treats and toys,

CHAPTER 9   Physical and Mental Exercise

or you can purchase a dog toy that simulates a digging area for your Scottie.

When outside, a simple sandbox can keep your Scottie occupied and out of your garden. Set up a DIY agility dog course in your backyard. You don't need fancy equipment as long as you have something your Scottie can run around to avoid or climb and jump over.

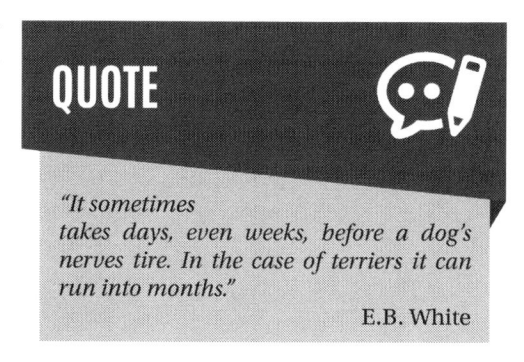

> **QUOTE**
>
> *"It sometimes takes days, even weeks, before a dog's nerves tire. In the case of terriers it can run into months."*
>
> E.B. White

All of these ideas can help keep your pup occupied, but don't forget the other members of your pack! If you properly socialize your other dogs or your cats, they can keep each other entertained while you're busy. My Beagle and my cats enjoy playing together, though the cats do have a limit to how much doggy play they can stand.

Make sure your Scottish Terrier knows how to play safely and nicely with your cats, and for the first few dog/cat playtimes, watch as your cats show your Scottish Terrier their boundaries for playtime. After you can be sure they're all playing nicely, you can trust your cats to keep your Scottish Terrier occupied.

CHAPTER 10
Clear Expectations

"Scotties are like cats. Ever trained a cat? Don't get frustrated, just have patience. Scotties are strong willed. Stay consistent with your training and you'll have a great dog."

Lainie Culton
Culton's Scottish Terriers

The most important part about training your Scottish Terrier, or any dog, is being clear about exactly what you want from your Scottie and being as clear as possible when communicating with her. Many owners complain that their dogs won't come when called or won't sit when commanded to, but the most common cause for this problem isn't that the dogs are being willfully disobedient; these dogs just don't understand what is expected of them because their owners haven't made their expectations clear enough.

Imagine if you were lost in a city where you didn't speak the language, and while in this city, you accidentally broke the law. You may have been warned against whatever action you took that got you the attention of local authorities, but if you didn't understand what was being said to you, those warning words weren't useful in keeping you out of trouble.

For dogs, clear expectations are even more important since they don't have the benefit of understanding human nonverbal communication to the extent that most humans do. A human can see from the angry faces and mummers of those around him that whatever he's done isn't good, but your Scottish Terrier will understand she's done something wrong only if you've made the difference between "right" and "wrong" clear to her in the first place. Otherwise, angry words will just frighten your pup because she won't understand that her behavior has caused your reaction.

To learn how to communicate clearly to your Scottish Terrier, first learn to understand how dogs communicate and what those communications mean. The two important communication methods for dog training are eye contact and tail position.

Eye contact with dogs conveys a few different things. On one hand, eye contact from your dog can show that she's affectionate toward you while

CHAPTER 10 Clear Expectations

avoiding eye contact can indicate that she is uncomfortable or feeling guilty. On the other hand, when you stare at your dog for too long, she may feel uncomfortable because staring can be challenge or a sign of dominance. If your Scottish Terrier is about to get herself into trouble by breaking a house rule, well-timed eye contact can remind her of her place.

Tails are your best friend when trying to understand your dog's mood. Your dog's tail will wag joyfully, swish cautiously, stand alertly, curve happily, droop sadly, or tuck anxiously. Watch your dog's tail to see what she's feeling so you can react appropriately to her mood. Clear communication between you and your Scottish Terrier is the basis of her successful training as well as the continued growth of your relationship with her.

Photo Courtesy of Brandon Holloway

Tracey SQUAIRE | The Complete Guide to Scottish Terriers

Photo Courtesy of
Verna Bardsley

CHAPTER 10 Clear Expectations

Hiring a Trainer/Attending Classes

Dog training can be tough, but it's also one of the first chances you'll have to socialize with your Scottish Terrier and to deepen the bond you have. The earlier you start training, the stronger the bond. When you hire a trainer to teach your Scottie her basic commands, you both miss out on this vital bonding time.

On the other hand, a dog trainer can help when you are too busy to train your dog yourself or if you aren't sure where to start with training. If you do go this route, be sure to spend plenty of time practicing and reinforcing what the trainer has taught your dog.

> **QUOTE**
> **Patience is a Virtue**
>
> Don't accept any behavior from a puppy that you would not tolerate in an adult dog. With consistent and positive training, your Scottish Terrier can learn nearly anything. The Scottish Terrier Club of America (scta.biz) encourages owners to "participate in activities such as agility, flyball, earthdog (terrier hunt tests), rally obedience" and more.

Attending a training class with your Scottish Terrier is better for you both since you'll gain dog-training knowledge together and will have a trainer on hand to correct both you and your dog during practice.

Remember that what a dog trainer and a training class provides is merely the tools for properly training your dog. Trainers and classes teach pet owners how to perform basic commands and how to interact with their dogs in the context of the class, but real life definitely won't be as structured as a dog-training class, so even if you attend classes for training, you will need to learn how to deal with behavioral issues and give commands as the situation dictates.

Owner Behavior

Your behavior toward and around your Scottish Terrier will dictate not only how well she learns her basic commands but also how likely she is to follow those commands. Dog training is mostly about teaching you, the owner, the commands to teach your dog as well as the proper techniques to use during training.

Daily practice of the commands you teach your Scottie is important to keep those commands fresh in your dog's brain. These commands can be used in many day-to-day situations. The sit and stay there commands are the most-used in my household, otherwise my Beagle would follow behind his favorite humans all day or trip up anyone who holds food. You can't be sure which commands you'll need your Scottish Terrier to know in any one moment, so regularly practice them daily or weekly.

Sadly, one of the most common reasons Scottish Terriers end up in shelters is that their original owners don't spend the time to properly train them and later find that the unruly pup is not to their liking. It's never too late to start training a dog, but some people won't put in the effort at any point in the dog's life.

CHAPTER 10   Clear Expectations

Operant Conditioning Basics

Operant conditioning in dog training is trial and error for your Scottie, who will understand the rules only after you've corrected her behavior. This method of training is useful for conveying basic concepts and is important early on in your Scottish Terrier's training because it's simple to understand for such a young mind being molded by another species.

Children who play with fire often feel the burn of experience, but that experience teaches them not to play with fire in the future and, perhaps, to be more careful around open flames. Those who are rewarded for positive behaviors later remember how they felt after being rewarded for that positive behavior and will use that memory when forming future behaviors.

Operant conditioning allows you to communicate to your Scottish Terrier when she has performed a behavior you find agreeable (peeing in the designated area, being respectful on walks) as well as when she has performed an action you find disagreeable (peeing on the carpet, pulling against the leash to run or chase).

The simplest way to communicate with a puppy is with rewards and punishments which are known in dog training as positive and negative reinforcements. Reinforcement refers to an event or action that strengthens or increases a behavior that follows. The behaviors are voluntary and are either strengthened or weakened by the resulting consequences.

Positive reinforcement increases the behavior by adding a reward or a punishment for a certain behavior. Positive reinforcement is the reason your Scottish Terrier will gladly sit when you ask her to because she remembers that she often gets treats when you ask her to sit.

Positive reinforcement can be used to add punishment as well, which many cats who walk on counters find out when their owners reinforce the "no pets on the counters" rule with a squirt of water to the hindquarters.

Negative reinforcement reduces the behavior by removing a favorable aspect in the dog's life or an unfavorable aspect in the dog's life. In dog training, negative reinforcement applies to the removal of a stimuli in order to increase a specific behavior.

The danger with negative reinforcement is that whatever stimuli you are removing to increase a behavior will be unpleasant to your dog. Some people use pinches or yells to get their dogs to follow commands. The removal of these unpleasant experiences ensures the dogs don't do whatever set their owners off again. But without clear communication, dogs may not

Photo Courtesy of Emmet Murphy

understand why they're in trouble and may develop anxiety about performing any action they think may trigger their owners again.

Dog whistles are examples of a negative reinforcement you can use with your Scottish Terrier, especially if you need to control her barking. She'll soon learn that stopping the noise from the whistle is as simple as stopping her barking.

This training method is all about aversion and is why electric fences can keep some animals from leaving their yards, but with negative reinforcement, the unpleasant stimulus has to be strong enough to reinforce the behavior. Electric fences simply don't work for Scottish Terriers because the shock isn't enough to bother them as they escape the yard.

Overall, reward-based training methods have been proven to work better not only for clearly communicating the desired behaviors but also for reinforcing those behaviors in the future. Negative reinforcement has the potential to breed anxiety and aggression in dogs who may be confused or just upset at the use of unpleasant stimuli.

When reinforcing your Scottish Terrier's behavior, you need to make what you're offering your Scottie in exchange for her changing her behavior worth her time. If your Scottie isn't a fan of toys, giving her a new toy when she's learned a new command will be somewhat disappointing and won't have her as excited to perform new commands as a meaty snack would.

CHAPTER 10   Clear Expectations

Primary and Secondary Reinforcements

Primary reinforcements are those a dog is born desiring or requiring such as sustenance, socialization, and shelter. Secondary reinforcers are those reinforcers your dog learns to desire such as a tasty treat, a good game of tug, or a belly rub.

Your Scottish Terrier needs to eat each day and have access to clean water, but smart owners know that they can work feeding and watering into their dog-training schedule. Receiving dinner can serve as a nice reward after your pup has successfully performed the sit command. Your Scottish Terrier will get her dinner and learn that following commands is rewarded.

Primary reinforcements that are basic necessities in your Scottish Terrier's life should not be withheld as a form of punishment. Withholding food or affection as a form of showing your Scottie your displeasure will confuse her without the use of clear communication and positive reinforcement to guide your Scottie toward displaying the appropriate behaviors.

Choosing to reward your Scottish Terrier with treats is an example of a secondary reinforcement. Your dog doesn't need treats to live, but treats are something she's learned to enjoy, and when you present her with yummy treats, you are reinforcing the positive bond between you along with whatever behavior she's learning.

Secondary reinforcements should be paired with primary reinforcements. Secondary reinforcements help increase the likelihood that the primary reinforcement will be successful in getting your Scottie to display the desired behavior. Secondary reinforcers get your dog's attention in an obvious way and say, "Hey, you did a good thing, and I want you to keep doing that good thing!" Your Scottish Terrier will get the message loud and clear when you reward her for digging in her own sandbox by giving her a new treat after she's had fun where you've shown her is appropriate.

With both primary and secondary reinforcers, it's vital that you continue the associations between training and reward. Training should be ongoing through your Scottish Terrier's life, even if that training is merely a review of skills your Scottie has already learned. Regular and consistent training likewise increases the reliability of the behavior so you won't be caught telling your Scottie to sit in front of guests only to have her stare at you quizzically.

CHAPTER 11
Basic Commands

"Do not get offended if your Scottie does not come when called. If you are new to the breed this can be frustrating. If you have had this breed before, you already know this!"

Lainie Culton
Culton's Scottish Terriers

Benefits of Proper Training

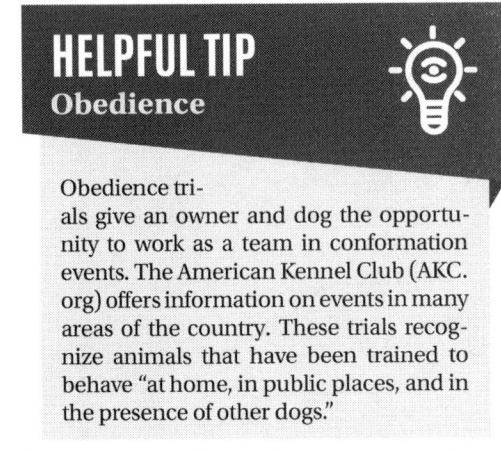

HELPFUL TIP
Obedience

Obedience trials give an owner and dog the opportunity to work as a team in conformation events. The American Kennel Club (AKC.org) offers information on events in many areas of the country. These trials recognize animals that have been trained to behave "at home, in public places, and in the presence of other dogs."

Properly training your dog presents many benefits, the most obvious of which is owning a well-trained dog who does what you ask when you ask. Having control over your Scottish Terrier could very well save her life or prevent an avoidable incident that would otherwise be outside of your control.

Besides the benefits of preventing bodily harm, proper training presents an opportunity for deep bonding between you and your dog. Dog training is not just you getting your dog to understand what you want. You should be using your dog-training sessions to understand how your Scottish Terrier communicates in order to better understand his individual personality.

Proper training provides a solid base for a well-socialized dog who communicates and interacts with humans and other animals in a calm and respectful manner. Additionally, your Scottish Terrier will enjoy the mental stimulation that accompanies training. Remember that Scottish Terriers are farm dogs; they're used to knowing and performing the tasks their owners put them to and enjoy doing those tasks well.

CHAPTER 11 Basic Commands

Picking the Right Rewards/Treats

Photo Courtesy of Roxane Deluna

The type of reward you give your Scottish Terrier is all about the skill you're teaching her. After your Scottie has had a long training session learning sit and stay, she may be ready for a game of fetch as a reward. Or perhaps it's the end of the day, and you want to end the sit and stay lesson with a *lie down* refresher by giving her something hard to spend 10 minutes chewing on while she spends time with the family in the main room.

Sometimes the reward you give your Scottie will be based on what she prefers. Some dogs prefer crunchier treats, and some like soft and meaty treats. Some dogs don't enjoy playing typical social-reward games. If your dog is particular about her interests, maybe she prefers stretching out in the sun to relax instead of playing tug. In that case, you may increase your use of treats as a method of reward.

Consistent training sessions with plenty of rewards and treats during and after are proven to increase the skill retention rate during the reinforcement process. As such, treats that are small and easily devoured are your best bet when training your Scottish Terrier. She'll eat the treat so quickly that her attention won't be gone long from the task at hand, and she'll be working her hardest to get one more tasty bite.

Photo Courtesy of Aaron Gordon

CHAPTER 11 Basic Commands

Different Training Methods

Positive Reinforcement

Positive reinforcement is the dog-training method most commonly used because it simply works. Positive reinforcement works best in the moment your dog displays the desired behavior. An immediate treat or praise from you will go a long way in getting your Scottie to respond in the same manner in the future. Training sessions using this method should be short, sweet, and uncomplicated. Be clear with your commands, reward often, and don't rely completely on treats as reinforcers. Make sure that everyone within your household is using the exact same commands, otherwise your Scottish Terrier will just be confused about what's being asked of her.

Mirror Training

Mirror training relies on the concept of "monkey see, monkey do." Your dog will learn a lot of things from those around her. Early socialization with calm and well-trained dogs can benefit your Scottie. In mirror training, your dog is learning by watching a human or another dog complete a task and be rewarded for that task. Through observation, she'll learn acceptable behaviors. Reinforce these acceptable behaviors by offering a reward when your Scottie mimics those behaviors.

Clicker Training

Clicker training involves using a device to indicate to your dog when she's displayed the desired behavior. Clicker training helps to eliminate confusion during dog training. It's best used with other forms of training since it's a powerful and easy way to communicate.

Pack Leader Training

Pack leader training, also known as dominance training, receives a lot of controversial feedback from dog behaviorists and dog owners. Some believe the use of dominance in dog training is outdated and should no longer apply to the training of modern dogs who have been bred physically and socially to live as human companions.

Dominance is often misunderstood in the context of dogs and their wolf ancestors. While a wolf pack does have an alpha who leads the pack, he does not need to display his dominance at every turn because the other members of the pack are his family members and already see him as the leader because he is a confident and sure provider for the pack.

The traditional alpha male behavior that is widely believed is based on research from an artificially created pack containing wolves with no relation to each other besides their shared "wolfness." In this context, the wolves fought for control to construct a leadership structure.

Pack leader training isn't necessarily even about showing dominance over your dog like it's thought the alpha wolf of a pack would. As a human, you can show dominance by being the rule setter and the reward giver.

Some owners resort to aggression and behavior they believe an alpha wolf would display toward a misbehaving member of the pack. The truth is that your dog will respond better to clear communication rather than a parody of wolf communication that the modern dog hasn't engaged in since our ancestors first began domesticating them.

Pack leader training is not a negative training method when it is fully understood and used correctly. Being a good pack leader simply means that you set fair rules and address the needs of each member of the pack. Pack leader training may be more useful when living with multiple animals, especially of differing species.

Relationship Training

This method of training combines other forms of training but focuses on building a relationship between dog and owner. I recommend this type of training for Scotties since this method can and often does lead to a deep bond between both parties.

Relationship training is an agreement and an understanding between you and your pet that you work together to beneficially coexist with each other. During relationship training, when your dog doesn't sit, she doesn't get punished. Instead, you figure out why she didn't sit. Was she distracted? Did she not understand the command? And you ask yourself what you can do to communicate better with your dog.

This relationship should be mutually beneficial; your Scottish Terrier is your companion and someone who provides you comfort, and in return for the companionship your Scottie offers, you teach her how to live among humans and accept her as a valued member of your pack. This method of training is good for those who want an individualized approach to training.

CHAPTER 11   Basic Commands

Basic Commands

To make life among humans easiest for your Scottish Terrier, she should understand the things you communicate to her. Whether in the privacy of your home or in a public arena, your Scottie will be ready to interact and socialize because you've respectfully and calmly interacted with her and taught her to be calm and respectful around others.

Young dogs are impressionable, so what you teach your Scottish Terrier in her youth will be reflected throughout her life. Puppies also have short attention spans, so keep individual training sessions between 10 and 15 minutes to avoid overwhelming your dog.

Focus

Getting and keeping your Scottish Terrier's focus is one of the most valuable commands for you and your dog to know and is one of the best ways to influence your dog toward calmness.

To teach focus, stand or sit in front of your Scottish Terrier. Grab one of her toys, preferably her favorite, and put the toy in front of your dog's face to catch her attention. Your own attention should be on your Scottie's face so you can catch the moment she looks away from the toy and to you.

Once your Scottish Terrier focuses her attention on you, give her verbal praise. Practice catching her attention a few times before adding a verbal command. Use this command when teaching other basic commands.

Sit

The sit command is one of the easiest to teach your Scottish Terrier, and all you need are treats and a quiet training space. You may consider leashing your dog to keep her attention better, but a boring and uninteresting training space should be enough to keep your Scottie's focus on the attention, treats, and praise you're offering in exchange for her learning.

The first step is to catch your Scottie's attention. Saying her name may be enough, but you can also just show her the treat you're offering. Once her attention is on the treat, she'll be ready to learn how to get the treat from you.

Hold the treat above your dog's nose but not high enough that she has to stand up to sniff it. Keep the treat low as you guide it from your dog's nose to behind her head. She should end up in a sitting position after looking up to follow the treat with her nose and eyes. If she does stand, bring the treat lower and back to guide her into the sitting position.

Photo Courtesy of
Ambre Bethoux and Jake Wehner

Say *sit* as your Scottie enters the sitting position, and reward her with praise and the much-awaited treat.

Lie Down

"Lie down" is best taught from the sit position. After telling your Scottie to sit, hold a treat over her nose and move your hand down, leading her nose to the ground and slowly pulling away from your dog's body until she's completely in a lying position (bottom and elbows fully on the ground). The moment she is in the correct position, praise her and give her the reward. To reinforce this command further, leave several treats on the ground or use slow-eating treats to keep your Scottish Terrier in this position longer. Before she gets up on her own, give her the release cue and another reward.

Stay

You should teach your Scottish Terrier the *stay* command in the same space you've taught the previous commands. After your Scottie has successfully sat or laid down for a few seconds, praise her and reward her with a treat.

Repeat this process, extending the wait until your pup receives her treat. Add in a verbal cue and an optional hand movement, and continue extending the time she holds her position.

Release

The *release* command or cue lets your dog know that she is now allowed to end the previous command you've given. Wait five to 10 seconds after giving the previous command before giving a verbal cue to leave a position such as sit, stay, and lie down. Pairing your command with a hand motion will make it more recognizable. Slowly build the wait time between the previous command and the release command.

Come

The *come* command should be associated with positive or neutral actions afterward. If your Scottish Terrier gets into trouble whenever you call her to you, she will put off coming, forcing you to keep pointlessly repeating yourself. If you've already used "come" a lot before punishing your Scottish Terrier with a reprimand or with an end to playtime, you should choose a new command word. Do NOT use your dog's name as she will learn to ignore it.

Teach the *come* command in a small area, and consider using a leash to keep your Scottie focused and easily recovered. You haven't yet taught the come command, so you don't want your dog to get away while you're trying to teach her.

When teaching *come*, you need to be interesting enough for your pup to come to you. Be down on your dog's level when teaching this skill, and use an excited or high-pitched voice when calling your Scottie to you. Toys that squeak will also attract her attention. The goal is to entice your Scottie to you so you can begin pairing the action with the come command.

Be patient, and start with a small amount of space between you if your Scottish Terrier seems to struggle with learning the command. After she's mastered *come* in a quiet area, move somewhere busier and with more distractions to continue her training.

Off/Down

The *off* command is used to teach your Scottie to keep her paws on the floor and off your legs. When your dog stands or jumps to lean on your legs, turn away from her and say *off*. Watch for times when your dog is about to jump. You should notice her taking her weight from her front paws and be prepared to step or turn away to prevent your Scottie from getting a foothold.

The *down* command is used to keep your Scottie off furniture. You'll want to lure her off the furniture with a treat while pairing the action with a command after a few practices. You can either wait for your dog to get on the furniture or practice with her by inviting her onto the furniture. This second method affords a more consistent understanding of the skills since your Scottie will learn to "get down" when you ask and not only when she's on furniture she isn't allowed on.

Give/Drop

To convince your Scottish Terrier to give or drop something, practice with toys and treats. Have a variety of toys for your Scottie to play with. Once she's got a toy, hold a treat next to her nose and say *give* or *drop*. Praise your Scottie once she's opened her mouth, and let her eat the treat. Pick up the toy while she's eating the treat, and continue practicing. You may have to cycle through toys if your pup is reluctant to pick up one she's already dropped. Practice this skill throughout the day when your pup isn't expecting to be asked to drop her toy.

Walk/Heel

This command is a must for those puppies who are so excited for their walks that they pull and tug the entire time you're walking. While some owners may be able to walk at the pace their dogs demand, others enjoy a comfortable and slow-paced walk with their furry companion.

First, consider where you want your Scottish Terrier to walk. Traditionally, your left side is where your dog would walk. If you walk alongside a busy road, though, you may want your Scottie to walk away from incoming cars.

Next, while holding a treat out of reach and sight at chest-level, call your Scottish Terrier to you while pointing to the side you want her to walk along.

CHAPTER 11   Basic Commands

Once she comes to your side, let her know she's done well with a verbal or auditory indication, then reward her with a treat.

After the first few practices, begin associating this command with the command word you choose. Regularly practicing *heel* and pairing it with other training will cement the skill in your dog's mind and help reduce leash-pulling.

Advanced Commands

The basic commands covered here are just the tip of the iceberg when it comes to skills your Scottish Terrier can learn, and there are even more advanced skills that build on those learned from the basic command training. Advanced skills help to exercise and strengthen your Scottie's intelligence and physical endurance.

Consider teaching your Scottish Terrier the following advanced skills:

- Roll over
- Spin
- Jump
- Stand up
- Play dead
- Shake hands
- Wave

CHAPTER 12
Dealing With Unwanted Behaviors

Understanding Bad Behavior in Dogs

Bad behavior in dogs isn't usually "bad" at all. Dog behaviors that are considered bad include digging, chewing, chasing, running away, begging, ignoring commands, jumping, barking, growling, biting, etc.

There are also behaviors that some owners consider bad while others don't. Bad behavior in dogs is what the owner considers bad. Remember that your Scottish Terrier won't understand or know what is "bad" unless you spend the time teaching her what she should and shouldn't do.

Many cases of bad behavior can be explained by a lack of training, too much energy, fear, anxiety, health problems, or a combination of many different reasons. Bad behavior is rarely caused by your dog purposely acting out, though a dog without guidance from a clear authority may decide to do as she pleases. Bad behaviors aren't usually "caused" by anything but rather are a symptom of a problem your dog doesn't know how to communicate other than with her natural behaviors.

Since dogs can't communicate with humans with words, you must learn to interpret what your Scottish Terrier's behaviors mean. When your Scottie is barking constantly while you're away at work, she isn't doing so because she enjoys annoying your neighbors. Instead, she may suffer from separation anxiety and may require conditioning to be comfortable being alone. Separation anxiety can also cause your Scottie to dig or chew while you're away.

On the other hand, digging, chewing, chasing, running away, and barking can be caused by simple boredom. If your dog has nothing to occupy herself with all day, she'll use the only tools she has at her disposal for entertainment.

Whatever the behavior you want to manage, you should watch to see when and why your Scottish Terrier is displaying that behavior so you can properly address the problem.

CHAPTER 12 Dealing With Unwanted Behaviors

Photo Courtesy of Amanda Vearnals

103

Bad Behavior Prevention and Correction

Teaching a behavior is much easier than correcting one, so the best way to prevent bad behavior is to make corrections early before those behaviors become a habit for your Scottish Terrier.

Spend time observing your Scottish Terrier. If the behavior you want to watch for occurs when you're not home, consider purchasing a nanny cam or other monitoring system. After you've discovered the reason for your Scottie's behavior, remove the motivation to partake in that behavior.

If your dog only ever barks when she's alone, consider hiring a dog sitter or take your pup to a doggy daycare when you need to leave the house. If the barking occurs whenever people walk past the house, keep the windows closed and your Scottie occupied in some other part of your home.

Don't yell at your Scottish Terrier when she barks. You can interrupt her with a single spoken word such as hey or quiet to let her know her behavior is unacceptable, but constantly yelling for her to be quiet will just result in more barking as your dog assumes you're joining in on her barking fun.

Chewing is another bad behavior you may notice, and it's a behavior to keep watch of not only because it's annoying but also because it can be dangerous. It's just a fact that dogs will chew; they don't have hands, and when they're bored, chewing keeps them occupied. There is, however, a problem with chewing when the object being chewed is not an appropriate chew toy.

Your Scottish Terrier may chew on the carpet, on cords, on grass, on her own tail, on paper towels, on shoes, or on literally anything she can get her teeth on. To prevent your dog from chewing on inappropriate items, ensure she has plenty of toys she's allowed to chew on so she doesn't even consider chewing on other things.

When you catch your Scottish terrier chewing on something she shouldn't be chewing, divert her attention to something she is allowed to chew on. Keep things like shoes, socks, cords, and other inappropriate chewables out of reach of your Scottish Terrier.

> **HELPFUL TIP**
> **Be Assertive**
>
> Don't allow your Scottie to get away with excessive barking, digging, or chewing. Be consistent and assertive when correcting unwanted behaviors. Allowing your dog's behavior to "slip" or go unchecked will reinforce bad manners. The first command to teach your Scottie is "come." As Scotties tend to run off, mastering this command can be a matter of life and death for your beloved pet.

CHAPTER 12 Dealing With Unwanted Behaviors

*Photo Courtesy of
Becky Bratten*

Biting, like chewing, is natural for dogs, but even though your pup may playfully nibble on your hand at times, teach her that interacting with humans with her mouth is dangerous and may lead to biting incidents. Dogs sometimes bite or nibble to get someone's attention, so teach your Scottie another way to get your attention, and avoid ignoring your dog when she's trying to communicate with you so she doesn't have to resort to biting.

Aggression is a common behavior for unsocialized dogs, and the way to correct aggression is to desensitize your Scottish Terrier to whatever is making him aggressive. If your Scottie barks every time another animal passes the house, consider having a neighborhood pet playdate so your Scottie can meet and get used to the animals who may walk past his territory. Another option is to spend time teaching and practicing the quiet command sitting by the window with your Scottie.

Aggression can also be caused by fear; in this case, keep an eye on your dog's behavior and remove her from fearful situations such as events with loud noises or areas that make her feel crowded with no escape. Desensitize her to these fear-inducing environments over time, but be careful not to overwhelm her or to let her aggression get out of control.

Photo Courtesy of Carol White

CHAPTER 12   Dealing With Unwanted Behaviors

Scottish-Terrier-Specific Bad Habits

Digging is one behavior you're almost guaranteed to deal with as the owner of a Scottish Terrier. Whether you live somewhere with a yard or just have a nice plush carpet good for digging, your Scottie will dig his paws in because the instinct to dig is so strong within the breed. Digging often occurs out of boredom, so prevent this behavior by keeping your Scottie entertained, and provide him an area for digging. Consider purchasing a digging mat for your Scottie.

Disobedience occurs in improperly trained dogs, but it's more obvious in dogs of high intelligence who will watch and learn what they can get away with if they aren't taught otherwise. You must teach your Scottie early on who is in charge by clearly communicating and enforcing the house rules. Without properly showing your authority and teaching your dog to respect you, your Scottish Terrier may become stubborn and overly dominant toward the other members of your household.

Defensiveness is common in Scottish Terriers. This behavior may display as unfriendliness or as aggression. Remember that Scottish Terriers typically bond with only one or two people. These dogs don't often get along with other animals without socialization, oftentimes because the Scottie may find the others annoying or bothersome. Your Scottish Terrier won't be afraid to show his dislike to those who bother him, but this behavior isn't always acceptable when your Scottie is just grumpy and unfriendly in general. Consider keeping your Scottish Terrier leashed around other animals, children, and strangers if you haven't yet socialized him with these groups.

A good solution for all of these problems as well as other common behavioral problems is to wear your Scottish Terrier out with exercise, walks, and plenty of playtime. A tired Scottie is less likely to get into trouble when you're not around, and a well-socialized Scottie shouldn't be bored enough to get into trouble.

Consistency with corrections is vital when fixing bad habits. Everyone in the household needs to be on the same page about what is and isn't acceptable behavior from your Scottish Terrier, and everyone should know how to correct her the same way every time the behavior occurs to avoid confusing her and prolonging the unwanted behavior.

Call in a professional if the behavior is too much to handle alone. If the behavior is one that may cause harm to your Scottish Terrier, another member of your pack, or someone else, you should seek professional help instead of letting the behavior worsen.

Photo Courtesy of Yvonne Kazan

CHAPTER 13
Traveling with Scottish Terriers

Dog Carriers and Car Restraints

Vehicles pose a lot of dangers to us and can pose higher dangers to our tiny pets, especially if those pets are improperly secured. Safety features for humans are built into cars by law, but dog owners must make additional purchases to ensure the safety of their animal companions when out on the road.

Without a car restraint or pet carrier, your Scottish Terrier may have access to roam the car at will, potentially distracting the driver, causing an accident, and causing injury to both himself and or others involved.

By purchasing a car restraint, you can be sure your Scottish Terrier is safe when you need to take him along on a drive. Car restraint options are

CHAPTER 13 Traveling with Scottish Terriers

varied; you can purchase anything from a special car harness kit to a simple buckle that can turn your Scottie's leash into a seat belt.

Another option for car travel is a dog carrier. Dog carriers are much more than convenience items or stylish accessories for the lucky small breeds who get to enjoy their comfort. Dog carriers are useful and recommended for car rides since they are designed to keep dogs comfortably contained and secured.

Dog carriers come in many different designs just like car restraints, so shop around before settling on one carrier. Keep in mind your own lifestyle; if you travel a lot and plan to take your Scottish Terrier on road trips, you may consider investing in a more expensive traveling pet bed that maximizes the safety and comfort of your Scottie. On the other hand, if the only travel your Scottie will experience is the ride to and from the vet, you may need just a sturdy carrier that you can safely secure in your car. Your Scottish Terrier will require a carrier around 30 inches tall.

Your dog carrier is useful for more than just travel. Sometimes, you may need your Scottie to be calm and confined to one area. Your dog carrier can be used to cart your pup along if you plan to make visits to other people's homes, or you may think to confine your Scottish Terrier to his carrier where he would be much safer during an emergency.

Photo Courtesy of Judy Chrzanowski

Photo Courtesy of Monique Dearlove

Preparing Your Dog for Car Rides

Your dog might fear cars and car rides for understandable reasons. For one, your Scottish Terrier may not be used to being inside of or around a giant metal machine that emits a strange smell and makes frightening noises. Your dog's senses are incredibly sensitive, so he needs to become used to the ways in which a car can stimulate his senses.

Even when your Scottie is inside your car, the battle may not be over. Your Scottish Terrier may become anxious if he is riding in the back seat alone, and just as many people suffer from motion sickness, so can dogs. Within your unfamiliar and swerving vehicle, your dog may experience nausea and vomiting and long-term negative associations with car rides may occur.

Whatever your goal with training your Scottie to be comfortable with car rides, you have a few options for making the ride easier on you and your Scottish Terrier.

Spend some time acquainting your dog with being around and inside your car. Depending on how nervous your dog is, this may take several conditioning sessions. Training your dog to be comfortable in a car will make both long and short car rides less stressful. Walk around your car with your dog on a leash, and let him sniff the tires and look under the car's body. Open all the doors to let him sniff the inside before entering.

CHAPTER 13   Traveling with Scottish Terriers

Next, head to the back door or the trunk if your car has a large enough space for your Scottie to travel comfortably. A dog restraint that blocks off and secures a section of your car may be a good option to give your pup more room to roam safely on long trips. Let your Scottish Terrier smell the area he's going to be spending most of his time in the car, then climb in and invite your dog to join you. If he's reluctant, be patient and let him take his time, and don't forget to use toys and treats! Once your pup is inside the car, praise him; he's just made an important step in life.

Spend time bonding with your dog inside the car. Go for a short drive around the block with your Scottie properly secured. Take a trip to a dog park or somewhere else especially rewarding. Each step you take with training your Scottish Terrier to become comfortable inside of a vehicle should be taken with patience and understanding.

Remember that exposing your Scottish Terrier to new situations is all part of the socialization process, and with continued exposure to car rides, your dog may come to love long cross-country drives where he can sleep and watch the world pass you by.

If it happens that your Scottie isn't the road-trip kind of dog and gets motion sickness, keep trips as short as possible. For longer trips, talk to your veterinarian about any medications that may help.

Packing and Preparing for a Car Ride

Whether you're heading to the vet or out of town, you need to prepare for the trip with your Scottish Terrier.

For shorter trips, a travel crate or carrier is usually all you need besides a leash. You can pack a water bottle and a few toys if you're expecting to be away long enough to need these items. If you're unsure whether your pup has done his business before you leave the house, take along doggy waste bags. Veterinarians and pet-store workers don't enjoy cleaning waste any more than we do.

For long trips, pack what you think you'll need for your ride. Thunder jackets are a consideration for especially anxious dogs. Clothes that smell like you will help to keep your Scottish Terrier calm during the ride, especially if he can't be close to you. Toys are a must for longer car rides as well as waste bags, food in a container, and drinkable water. You may also purchase some nonmedicated calming supplements to help calm your anxious dog.

Before a car ride, exercise your Scottish Terrier so he'll be calmer during the ride. A mild walk is sufficient. Avoid feeding or watering your pup before a trip to prevent motion sickness and potty accidents on the road.

Flying and Hotel Stays

When you're traveling with your Scottish Terrier, you may need to stay at a hotel. Unfortunately, not every hotel or motel is dog friendly, so as with many things in life, research and planning are required for an uncomplicated trip to happen. Researching pet-friendly hotels is as simple as using a filter on your chosen GPS map app, but not every pet-friendly hotel is equal.

Some hotels will require that your pet be declared during the room registration process and kept on a leash whenever he leaves the room, and some hotels charge a nonrefundable fee and may charge additional "cleaning fees" for longer stays, while others won't charge you at all for spending a night at their hotel with your furry family member.

Most hotels allow no more than two dogs with the total weight of one or both of the dogs not exceeding 80 pounds and won't allow you to leave your Scottie alone in your room. Whatever the policy, check what you are and aren't allowed to do before hitting the road with your Scottish Terrier. Motel 6, La Quinta Inn, and Holiday Inn are some popular chains which typically allow pets.

Begin introducing your Scottish Terrier to new places as early as possible, and while in these new places, train your dog to pee and poop on command. Training your Scottie to do his business on command will save you a lot of time watching your Scottie nervously sniff an unfamiliar area before deciding to do his business safely in the hotel room which at least smells somewhat familiar. See Chapter 11 to learn how to train your Scottie to pee on command.

A dog carrier is a smart item to pack for longer rides, especially if you plan to stay at a hotel. You can use the carrier to keep your Scottish Terrier out of the way as you unpack your car and enter your room, or you can allow him to sleep in the carrier, securing it at night to prevent any marking inside the room. Though it isn't recommended, if you need to keep your pup out of trouble while you're gone for a short while, you can contain your Scottish Terrier in his carrier.

More and more hotels are becoming less pet friendly because of barking complaints, and it's the responsibility of dog travelers everywhere to ensure that their dogs feel safe, are comfortable, and aren't disturbing other travelers. If the only way to accomplish those goals is to follow the rules hotels set and avoid leaving your Scottish Terrier alone, it may be worth the extra effort to keep hotels all over pet free and keep pet fees as low as possible.

Keep in mind that most dogs will bark when anxious, and being in an unfamiliar place, not knowing when your owner will return or whether he or she will return at all, is an incredibly stressful situation. Even though the pet carrier is an option if you absolutely must leave your Scottish Terrier alone, realize that your dog will bark regardless and disturb the guests around you.

When flying, you absolutely want to have a carrier if you want your Scottish Terrier to ride in the airplane cabin with you instead of being stuck in the cargo hold. You can contact your chosen airline to check if your Scottie and his carrier are small enough to ride with you inside the cabin.

> **HELPFUL TIP**
> **And a Small Dog ...**
>
> Can I travel internationally with my pet? Check with your airline and the country you are visiting for information about size and weight restrictions, vaccination certificates, and breed limitations. Will your dog be allowed to travel in the cabin or relegated to the cargo bin? Discuss pet flying fees which can range in price from $100-$300 depending on the airline.

The carrier you choose for your Scottish Terrier should be waterproofed or supplied with puppy pads, should close or zip completely, and should have plenty of ventilation since even if your Scottie does sit with you inside the plane, his carrier may be stored under the seat in front of yours.

Some preplanning is required to ensure your dog travels comfortably. Aim for middle seats since they typically have more under-seat storage space compared to aisle seats and window seats. You may want to do a few simulations with your pup to get him used to being in his crate in a small area for what could be hours at a time. If your dog is known to panic in such conditions, seek advice from a veterinarian who can prescribe a sedative if conditioning doesn't help.

Kenneling vs. Dog Sitters

Kenneling your dog is a good option if your dog prefers to be around other animals rather than to be alone. Even though Scottish Terriers are independent dogs, they still like to be around a pack, so if your Scottie isn't a cranky loner, be sure to find a kenneling service nearby to house him.

Kenneling services are helpful because the new pack your dog is temporarily invited into will help distract him from some of the anxiety he has from being away from you. Modern kenneling services offer open areas that facilitate play between the dogs.

Tracey SQUAIRE | The Complete Guide to Scottish Terriers

Photo Courtesy of Nichola Hennessey

Modern kenneling services are really just doggy daycares, and you can be picky about exactly which kenneling service you use for your dog, but if you have some reservations about kenneling, you can opt for a dog sitter instead.

A pet sitter is someone who either houses your dog in their home while you're away or will take care of your dog within your own home. Casual pet sitters are those such as your neighbor or a trusted friend who agree to watch your pup. Casual sitters are more likely to pet sit in their own homes for convenience. Professional pet sitters are more likely to visit your home periodically throughout the day as they make their rounds to other dogs they take care of. A pet sitter will visit your home several times a day to feed, socialize, and walk your dog.

Again, which service you choose depends on the needs of you and your Scottish Terrier.

Tips and Tricks for Traveling

Before traveling by plane or car, don't forget to visit your veterinarian to ensure a clean bill of health for your dog. Depending on where you travel, you may need to provide evidence of your dog's health and vaccination records, so keep these items on hand so there's no trouble at the airport or when crossing borders. Certification of your dog's good health should be provided to the airline at least 10 days before your scheduled flight.

You can keep medical papers inside of your dog's travel kit which should include toys and games to keep him occupied, pet identification papers in case he gets lost, and any medications your dog may need during the trip such as regular medications or sedatives prescribed specifically for the trip.

It's smart to set and keep a feeding schedule on the road. Most travelers find that their dog's normal feeding schedule is best. Keeping your dog's normal feeding and bathroom schedule can help your Scottish Terrier feel a sense of familiarity, thereby reducing his levels of anxiety.

Keeping his same feeding schedule also allows you to keep his potty schedule about the same, so you should be able to predict when you need to make stops. In fact, you should check out your route before starting your trip to identify dog-friendly areas at which to stop. Exposing your Scottie to these new areas is all part of socialization!

Remember, don't leave your Scottish Terrier alone in a vehicle. Anything can happen while you're away, even if you believe your dog is safe and comfortable in your car for just a few minutes.

CHAPTER 14
Nutrition

Importance of Good Diet

Photo Courtesy of Michelle Lynch

All animals require a specific balance of nutrients to keep their bodies functioning how they were designed to, and your Scottish Terrier is no different. An unbalanced diet for your Scottie can cause problems such as obesity or weight loss, skin disease, low energy, moodiness, and acting out.

Poor nutrition can be caused by a lack of food or a lack of quality food. Medical conditions can also cause poor nutrition if that condition limits the desire to eat or limits the absorption of vital nutrients. Intestinal parasites are a major cause of poor nutrition as they consume nutrients before your dog's body is able to absorb those nutrients.

Your Scottish Terrier's diet should not stay the same throughout her life since there are different dietary needs for different life stages. It's important to consult a veterinarian at different points in your Scottie's life to get advice on what kind of food to feed your companion.

CHAPTER 14   Nutrition

Balanced Nutrition for Your Dog

Your Scottish Terrier requires a mix of proteins, carbohydrates, fatty acids, vitamins, and minerals in the food she eats every day. Without the regular ingestion of these nutrients, your dog's body won't be able to work how it was built to work. Simply put, your Scottish Terrier needs to eat, and she needs to eat quality ingredients! Even though her body is small, it is still made up of a lot of muscles that your Scottie uses every day to run, jump, and play.

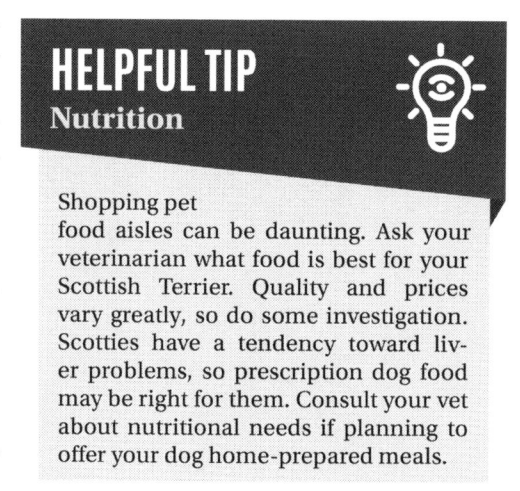

> **HELPFUL TIP**
> **Nutrition**
>
> Shopping pet food aisles can be daunting. Ask your veterinarian what food is best for your Scottish Terrier. Quality and prices vary greatly, so do some investigation. Scotties have a tendency toward liver problems, so prescription dog food may be right for them. Consult your vet about nutritional needs if planning to offer your dog home-prepared meals.

All that exercise burns a lot of calories, and depending on your Scottie's activity level, life stage, or pregnancy status, she may require between 709 and 1575 calories a day to maintain her health. Specific dog foods are made for different life stages, and your veterinarian can suggest an appropriate food based on your dog's specific needs.

Proteins are most important for very young animals or animals in stages of growth. A pregnant Scottish Terrier or one younger than 8-10 months should eat a dog food high in protein to support the growth and changes their bodies will go through.

Protein is a vital ingredient in the building and structure of the body including skin and hair cells, muscles and tissues, and internal organs. Without proteins, your Scottie will be unable to build and maintain muscle mass.

Carbohydrates are just as important as proteins in your dog's diet, though that fact has been hotly debated by those who would prefer to keep their dog's diet as close to a wolf's diet as possible, but dogs are not wolves and have their own dietary needs based on how their bodies have developed alongside humanity's.

Carbs are vital in the modern dog's nutrition. The first dogs scavenged the scraps and leftovers found around human encampments, meaning they had access to carbohydrates from plants, grains, fruits, and vegetables. The modern dog's body reflects the changes those ancient wolves made to become the dogs we know today.

Photo Courtesy of
Jada Blankenship

Carbohydrates provide a quick source of energy since carbs are usually very easy to digest. Since dog foods contain a mix of nutrients, not all of them will be absorbed all at once; carbs help your dog get energy now to engage in regular activities as well as to digest those other sources of energy. Besides being an important source of energy, carbs in kibble give it a texture that's easily chewed by dogs and helps with controlling tartar build up and provides a source of fiber.

Essential fatty acids contribute to the health and quality of your Scottish Terrier's skin and coat, but these nutrients also help maintain the structure of smooth muscle organs such as the heart. Dogs eating a diet rich with fatty acids will have shiny fur. The most common category of fatty acids important to a dog's health are omega-6 and omega-3. Sources of these essential fatty acids are foods such as seeds, vegetables, fish, and some meats.

Vitamins are vital for many different aspects of your dog's health including vision health, immune health, bone health, and more. Certain vitamins are necessary for the absorption of other vitamins, so a balanced mix of vitamins in your dog's diet is essential. Minerals are no different as they support the growth of bones and teeth and provide other nutritional benefits that contribute to the overall health of your dog.

Signs and Symptoms of Improper Nutrition

Sometimes, it's hard to notice when we as humans are missing a nutrient in our diets. We may have a general feeling of illness that we can't quite pinpoint or have aches that come out of nowhere. With dogs, the same may be true, but they cannot tell their owners these things. You must recognize what "normal" behavior is for your Scottie so you can realize when something is wrong.

Fortunately, there are some physical signs of malnutrition you can watch for to ensure your Scottish Terrier's health.

A protein deficiency is caused by the body's failure to absorb enough protein either because it just isn't present in the diet or because something is blocking absorption. Protein deficiency can cause weight loss, a decrease in muscle mass, difficulty breathing, weakness, or a lack of energy in an otherwise energetic pup.

While your Scottish Terrier does need protein, she can have too much in her diet. An excess of protein can cause your dog's kidneys to work harder as the unused proteins cannot be absorbed for normal bodily functions and will be filtered out through the kidneys or stored as extra fat, causing weight gain.

A deficiency of essential fatty acids can cause scaly skin, hair loss, a dull coat, digestive problems, degenerative eye disease, and cardiovascular disease. You may notice dandruff, ear infections, or excessive itchiness.

The anti-inflammatory benefits these fatty acids provide also reduce itchy and dry skin caused by environmental factors such as dry or cold air, though too much of these fatty acids can negate the positive effects and cause inflammation as well.

Itchiness may not seem like a big deal, but constant scratching can drive both you and your pup crazy and may give guests the impression that your home may be infected with fleas when, instead, she's getting too much or too little of the nutrients meant to keep her coat and skin healthy.

Too few carbohydrates in your Scottie's diet can result in low energy since carbs are a quick source of fuel.

Even though carbohydrates play a role in your Scottie's energy levels, some dog foods supply more carbohydrates than your dog may actually need. Dog foods can be composed of between 30 and 70 percent carbohydrates. With too little exercise or a predisposition toward weight gain, a diet high in carbohydrates can be detrimental to your dog's health.

A lack of adequate vitamins and minerals can cause lethargy, muscle pain, trembling, eye disease, heart failure, and more, depending on the missing nutrient.

These conditions can be caused by under- or overfeeding, lack of quality food, food allergies, intestinal worms, bowel diseases, cancer, heart failure, or any number of other conditions. Your veterinarian can diagnose and advise you on treatments for whatever is causing these symptoms; it's important that you observe your dog regularly for changes in activity, behavior, appearance, food consumption, and bowel movements.

Besides medical conditions or infections that can prevent or drain these vital nutrients, your Scottish Terrier shouldn't have the chance to become malnourished as long as she is regularly eating commercial dog food, which is required by the FDA to meet a variety of basic nutritional needs for dogs. Not all dog foods are created equally, though, and some may have a higher concentration of some vitamins or nutrients than others.

CHAPTER 14   Nutrition

Good Foods for Scottish Terriers

Puppies naturally need more energy to support their growth and development, but Scottish Terriers young and adult burn a lot of calories like many other small-dog breeds, so a food high in both protein as well as carbs is essential to provide these pups with the fuel they need to get through a day of defending your home.

> **FUN FACT**
>
> The Scottie has been the most popular Monopoly playing piece since the 1950s.

When searching for a dog food for your Scottish Terrier, you want to look for quality ingredients. Proteins should come from an animal, and that animal should be named. A simple label of "meat protein" is too vague and should set off red flags. Carbs are a must, especially for puppies, but make sure that the amount of carbs in your dog's diet reflects the life stage she's in as well as her activity levels.

Fatty acids will be labeled a variety of ways, but they are typically labeled as omega-3 and omega-6. Just ensure that there are indeed essential fatty acids, but be aware that omega-3 has a shorter shelf life than other fatty acids and may not be as potent as the dog food label claims.

A balanced diet for your dog should include vitamins A, B, C, D, E, K, as well as the vitamin choline. Trace minerals such as iron, zinc, magnesium, copper, and iodine are also something to look out for on the ingredients list.

Other than the above nutrients, you want to ensure that the food your dog is eating is made with quality ingredients. Many of the nutrients listed can come from several sources, not all of which will be healthy or easy for your Scottish Terrier to ingest.

The inclusion of vegetables and fresh ingredients in general is a good sign. Some dog foods even include nonessential nutrients such as probiotics or extra fiber. The specific nutrients you want to look for depend on your Scottish Terrier's age, activity level, and health. You can consult your veterinarian or an animal nutritionist to find the right diet for your Scottish Terrier.

Different Types of Commercial Food for Small Dogs

Puppies

Canidae Life Stages Chicken & Rice Formula is a wet dog food that can stay in your pantry throughout your Scottie's life. Since the formula is made for different stages of a dog's life, your Scottie shouldn't have to go without a familiar food just because she happens to be getting older. This food is appropriate for puppies, adults, and seniors.

Wellness Small Breed Complete Health Puppy Turkey, Oatmeal & Salmon Meal Recipe aims to give your Scottie the most out of each meal. With turkey as a source of quality protein and carrots as protection against eye and heart disease, this formula is designed to meet the specific health needs of small dogs like your Scottie.

Free of artificial flavors and colors, **Hill's Bioactive Recipe Grow + Learn Chicken & Brown Rice Puppy Dry Food** is easily digestible to make the most of the nutrients provided. This formula is made without corn, wheat, and soy and is made with apples as a source of antioxidants.

Canidae Under the Sun Grain-Free Puppy Food is a good choice for those who want a higher-protein, lower-carb diet for their companions. The grain-free formula contains probiotic, antioxidants, and farm-grown fruits and vegetables. This recipe does not contain red meat or potatoes.

Whole Earth Farms Grain-Free Puppy Recipe is another quality high-protein option. The formula is meant to bring the best of what earth has to offer to your dog's bowl. The recipe is made to be easily digestible and support a shinier coat with less shedding. Chicken and salmon proteins provide all the energy your puppy needs to grow and play.

Adults

Hill's Science Diet Dry Dog Food, Adult, Small Paws for Small Breeds, Lamb Meal & Brown Rice Recipe is enhanced to provide precise and balanced nutrition. The formula is designed to support a long life for small dogs and is clinically proven to support bone and muscle strength, digestion, and healthy immune function.

With Rachael Ray's Nutrish Little Bites Small Breed Natural Dry Dog Food, Real Chicken & Veggies Recipe, you can give your Scottish Terrier a happy and full belly along with energy for her small but muscled body.

This formula is made with cranberries, which are high in antioxidants and may reduce stress levels.

Blue Buffalo Homestyle Recipe Natural Adult Small Breed Wet Dog Food contains high-quality chicken that provides essential amino acids. Whole grains such as brown rice and barley give your Scottie a source of carbohydrates for quick energy, and the fruits and garden vegetables provide a rich mix of nutrients. This recipe is free of wheat and soy products and does not contain artificial flavors or preservatives.

Halo Holistic Chicken and Chicken Liver Recipe for Small Breed Dogs is an easily digestible kibble small enough to fit the tiny mouth of your Scottish Terrier. Halo delivers a deliciously nutritious meal with its premium protein that never contains any animal byproduct. Halo products include the brand's own DreamCoat nutrient mix designed to support smooth skin and a shiny coat.

Nature's Recipe Grain Free Dry Dog Food Small Breed Chicken, Sweet Potato & Pumpkin formula is made to be easily digestible. With real chicken as the first ingredient, you can be sure your Scottish Terrier is getting protein from a quality source. Natural sweet potato and pumpkin offer a grain-free source of carbohydrates, and the formula contains copper and zinc proteinate to help maintain a healthy coat.

Seniors

Another option for all your Scottie's life stages, **Canidae All Life Stages Less Active Formula Dry Dog Food** is made specifically for dogs who are less active, overweight, or senior. The recipe contains a lower mix of fat but contains the brand's personal HealthPLUS Solutions mix of probiotics, antioxidants, and essential fatty acids.

Ultra Senior Dog Food is a safe option for older dogs who have food allergies. The formula is free of wheat and corn and uses rice grain to provide fiber for easier digestion. Ultra dog food contains proteins from chicken, lamb, and salmon. The recipe contains superfoods such as blueberries, chia, coconut, and kale.

Nature's Variety Instinct Raw Boost Senior is a grain-free dry food option full of protein and is specially formulated to support joint and immune health. This kibble is raw, retaining many of the essential nutrients inside. The recipe contains freeze-dried raw meat as a special treat for your aged Scottie warrior.

With a complete and balanced offering of nutrients in this dry food, **Wellness Small Breed Complete Health Senior Deboned Turkey &**

Photo Courtesy of Ambre Bethoux and Jake Wehner

Peas Recipe is a great option for the salt-sensitive elder Scottie. The formula focuses on heart health and weight maintenance for older dogs who've packed on a few pounds.

Another grain-free option for your elder Scottish Terrier is **Instinct by Nature's Variety Original Grain-Free Recipe with Real Chicken.** This recipe is full of real, cage-free chicken as the first ingredient. Seventy percent of this recipe is animal ingredients and healthy oils with the remaining 30% being fruits, vegetables, and other nutrients.

Feeding During Pregnancy

Pregnancy and nursing are times when you need to pay special attention to your Scottish Terrier's diet. Your Scottie will be giving much of her nutrients to her puppies before and after the birth. Malnutrition during pregnancy can lead to health problems for both the expectant mother as well as her unborn pups.

Pregnant dogs need more food later in the pregnancy compared to the first few weeks, and as her appetite increases, so too will the amount of food she consumes. Consult your vet on how much to feed your specific dog. You can purchase a food with more proteins and fats to ensure your Scottie has all the nutrients she needs for her pregnancy, but typically you can just increase the amount of her regular food.

Pregnant dogs have a tendency to lose their appetites, so you may want to switch to a wet food or moisten her food during this time. Allow her to eat as much as she wants during this time, and do what you can to make her food as appetizing as possible. Look for foods that are easily digested as these foods provide the most nutrient absorption.

CHAPTER 14   Nutrition

Subscription Services, Homemade Foods, Recipes

Many owners want their dogs to enjoy the same type of fresh, quality ingredients they themselves eat, so they invest money or time into subscription services or homemade dog food recipes.

Not every pet food company can be trusted. Even if it has previously had a clean record, the claims on the labels could be false, or the food might just not work for your Scottie.

Making dog food at home isn't hard, but it is vital to know what you're doing; not just any food can be given to dogs, and even the food that your dog can eat needs certain nutrients added to it to address all of your dog's dietary needs.

You can find free dog food recipes online or purchase a recipe book. Although not every meal needs to have every nutrient as long as you are feeding diverse recipes, in general, you want to include the following nutrients in the different foods you make at home for your Scottish Terrier:

- Meat and animal products
- A source of calcium
- A source of vitamin D
- Fruits, vegetables, leafy greens
- A source of carbs
- Cod or salmon oil
- A source of vitamin E

It's important that you consult your veterinarian or a licensed pet nutritionist before making drastic changes to your dog's diet. A nutritionist can provide you with a full list of all the vitamins and nutrients to include in the food you make for your Scottish Terrier and can also recommend specific sources of nutrients and places to buy supplements.

If you don't have time to cook your dog's food, you can purchase a subscription to receive fresh food delivered directly to your home. Since this trend of having fresh food delivered is becoming more and more popular for humans and animals alike, there are many options to choose from. Fresh dog food can help improve your dog's coat and skin, energy levels, and digestion.

People Food – Harmful and Acceptable Kinds

People food can serve as a suitable treat for your pet once in a while, but most foods humans eat are processed, over-salted, or otherwise contain ingredients that are detrimental to the long-term health of dogs.

To keep your Scottish Terrier healthy, limit how much of your own food you share. Besides the food mentioned in Chapter 3, you should avoid feeding your Scottie human food in general unless that food is prepared in a recipe suitable to meet your dog's nutritional needs. It would be unwise to waste your dog's daily caloric intake on foods that won't provide the other nutrients she needs.

That isn't to say your Scottie doesn't deserve a special treat that doesn't provide anything other than tastiness, but be aware that some "safe-to-eat" human foods, especially in excess, can cause health problems. Bread is a food that can definitely be high in carbohydrates and can cause weight gain. Ham is an acceptable snack, but its high sodium levels aren't ideal for it to be a regular treat.

Fat trimmings and other fatty foods can cause liver and pancreas problems. The liver is responsible for aiding digestion and removing toxins from the body. Treatment can be anything from a change of diet to medication to surgery. The meaty taste of animal fats just isn't worth the risk of permanently damaging your dog's liver. Cheese is a food that can be a good treat for your dog but can also be high in fat.

Weight Management

While the breed typically weighs between 19-22 pounds, there certainly will be Scottish Terriers who are either bigger or smaller than the breed standards. With that in mind, whether your Scottie is overweight shouldn't be decided just by what the scale says. Your veterinarian will warn you when your Scottie is hitting an unhealthy number on the scale, but you can notice for yourself when you need to reduce treats and increase walks.

To see if your Scottie needs to shed a few pounds, attempt to locate her ribs with your hands. You should be able to feel the outline of the rib cage without feeling extra flesh. If you can't find your Scottie's rib cage, it's time to consult your vet about a diet and exercise plan.

Remember that "overweight" isn't "obese," and the sooner you realize that your pup needs a lifestyle change, the easier it will be to guide her health back to where it should be. If your Scottie is prone to weight gain, consider purchasing a scale for frequent weight tracking. You can weigh yourself, then weigh yourself holding your dog to figure out how much she weighs. Just subtract your weight from you and your dog's combined weight.

Scottish Terriers are prone to obesity, so you should be conscious of the portion sizes you feed your pet. Use treats smartly during times such as training; training can involve physical exercises that help burn off the calories from those treats, and keeping treats to training sessions can help reduce begging because your Scottie will learn that she needs to earn her treats. Just make sure you can resist begging if and when it does happen.

Diet and exercise are the simplest ways to control your Scottie's weight, but if your Scottish Terrier is too overweight to exercise, you should definitely seek medical advice.

CHAPTER 15
Grooming Your Scottish Terrier

"While your Scottie is still a puppy, take clippers and go over their body with the back side of the clippers. This will get him or her use to the sound and sensation of the clippers at an early age, and make them more comfortable with grooming as they get older."

Jane Herron
Herron's Sandhills Scotties

Photo Courtesy of Ambre Bethoux and Jake Wehner

Regularly grooming your dog is important since she can't groom herself. Long-haired dogs like your Scottie require more regular grooming, so implementing a routine can help you keep up with all of your dog's grooming needs. Your grooming routine will change as you learn more about your dog's specific needs.

Your Scottish Terrier has an especially long coat that can become easily tangled and dirty if not kept up. Grooming encompasses more than just the coat, though. You must maintain coat length, coat cleanliness, nail length, teeth health, and ear and eye health.

It sounds like a lot of maintenance, but grooming can very easily be scheduled either all at once or at different times to keep you and your Scottish Terrier from doing too much at once and becoming overwhelmed.

When Professional Help is Necessary

Since your Scottie will need frequent grooming, you might want to do this grooming at home to save money, but there are definitely other reason a professional is the best choice to meet your grooming needs. Grooming can take a lot of time and energy, but you can take your pet to a professional groomer or hire one to come to your home.

A groomer will have all the tools necessary to keep your dog looking and feeling her best. You can buy all these tools yourself, but then you must dedicate the time that it takes to use those tools. A groomer has tools you may not even think to use or have time to use such as a variety of nail clippers and an adjustable grooming table, which may be useful for dogs with specific physical needs.

> **HELPFUL TIP**
> **Many Choices**
>
> Be prepared with pictures you've found on the internet when taking your Scottish Terrier for grooming. Whether you choose a puppy cut, show cut, or regular Scottie cut, shaving is never advised. Your dog has a two-layer coat that insulates him from the cold of winter and the heat of summer.

A dog groomer will work with your schedule, so all you have to do is make sure your dog is at the right place at the right time. You can let someone else do the hard work of trimming your dog's coat, cutting her nails, cleaning her ears, and shampooing her fur.

Older dog owners or those with disabilities may find the task of grooming to be too physically demanding, especially when the dog in question is young, full of energy, or anxious about the grooming process. Professional groomers know exactly how to handle dogs, anxious or calm, and they can be gentle with dogs who are injured or older.

There are also some tasks you may just prefer a groomer attend to. You may do regular grooming at home, but if your Scottish Terrier becomes infected with ticks or fleas or gets into something especially stinky, you can just take her to the groomer, and she'll be as clean as the day you brought her home when you see her again.

Tracey SQUAIRE | The Complete Guide to Scottish Terriers

Coat Basics

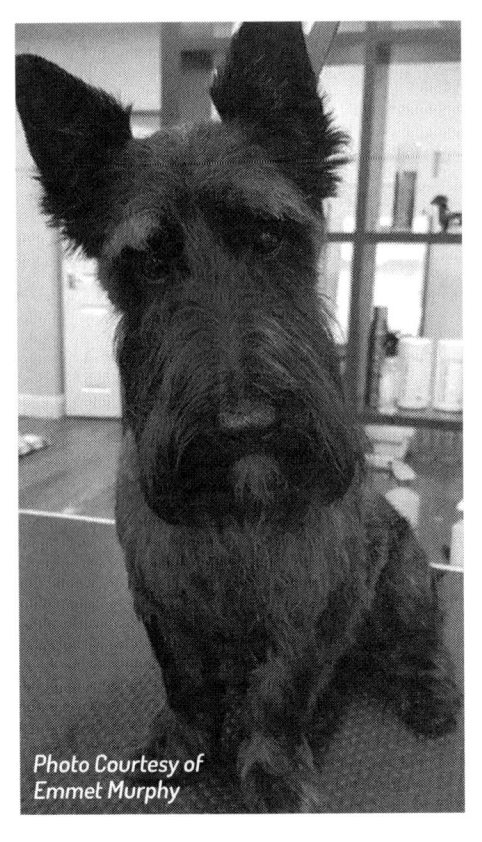

Photo Courtesy of Emmet Murphy

Scottish Terriers have a variety of coat grooming styles to choose from, although if you're cutting your Scottie's fur at home, you may want a style that is simple and quick to achieve.

The length you cut your dog's coat depends on the desired style, the season, temperature sensitivities, as well as your dog's comfort. For cutting your dog's fur, you can either use a comb and scissors or invest in hair clippers. Brush your Scottie's fur before cutting away fur so you can properly see what needs to be cut.

If you're content to regularly groom your dog at home, make sure you have all the tools you need to get the job done. Grooming at home doesn't have to be too arduous a task, especially if you plan for the situation. A simple grooming schedule can ensure that you aren't forgetting to take care of your dog's grooming needs, and making sure you have the tools made specifically to complete the job will make the whole process easier and faster.

Bathing and Brushing

Select the area you will frequently bathe your Scottie in. Make sure this area has somewhere for the end of your dog's leash to be attached because you definitely want to keep her on a leash to keep her focused and not running away. This area can be in the laundry room, the bathroom, an outside area, or any other area in your home that fits your needs.

For bath time, you'll want the following tools:

CHAPTER 15 Grooming Your Scottish Terrier

- Pet-friendly shampoo (human shampoos can strip the natural oils from your dog's fur)
- 1-3 towels, depending on how much water your dog fur holds
- A sink, tub, or kiddie pool to bath her in
- A water hose or pitcher of water
- *Optional* A blow dryer to make the drying process quicker
- A wide-toothed comb or dog brush

For a successful bath time, consider purchasing a lick mat on which you can smear peanut butter for your dog to distract herself with during baths. Your Scottish Terrier will be too distracted with the hard-to-eat yummy treat to be anxious. Bathing should occur about once every three months, but plenty of events can increase this schedule such as exposure to unsanitary areas outside. Consider investing in a spray-on pet shampoo for regular dog smells that may be unpleasant.

Photo Courtesy of Michelle Lynch

Brushing should occur after your Scottie is completely dry, but after a bath isn't the only time you should brush her fur. Your Scottie may love the bonding you two experience as you brush her, and the slow and relaxing brushing may be a comfort to her.

Brushing helps to remove built-up dirt and other debris as well as to stimulate natural oil production that aids in the health and look of your dog's coat. Brushing should occur at least once a week, but daily brushing can help reduce shedding and stop your furniture from being covered in pet hair.

Trimming the Nails

You should trim both the nails as well as the fur around your dog's nails. Use a pair of scissors to cut the fur down in this area.

Trimming your dog's nails may be a little stressful for both of you, especially the first few times you do it. Tools you'll need include nail scissors or a nail grinder if you prefer grinding. You should also have styptic powder or cornstarch on hand in case you cut too far on your dog's nail and injure the quick—the nerve or blood vessel in the nail.

You may need to get your dog used to you holding his paw and nails before getting started. Use treats to make your dog comfortable and to associate this process with positive things. Start slowly with one nail at a time, and consider breaking the trimming into multiple short sessions throughout the day.

If you're using a grinder, gently tap the grinder against your dog's nail until it gets to the desired length. Don't hold the grinder on the nail since you may grind away more than intended, and the grinder may heat to the point of pain for your pup.

If using nail scissors, position the nail inside the opening of the scissors and cut, making sure the blade isn't near the quick, which will look pink if your dog's nails are clear. If your dog's nails are black, recognizing the location of the quick will be harder. You may need to trim the nails regularly to ensure the quick doesn't grow past a certain point, or you may just leave the nail trimming to a professional for you and your dog's comfort.

If the quick has grown too far down your dog's nail for you to safely trim it, take your pet to the vet or to a groomer who can slowly cut the nail down until the quick recedes.

Brushing Their Teeth

Many people forget about dental care with dogs, especially since it's well known that dry kibble helps prevent tartar buildup, but dry kibble is not nearly enough to keep your Scottish Terrier's teeth healthy throughout his entire life.

Teeth cleaning should occur between three to seven times a week. Dental disease can lead to problems with other organs in the body if infections from the mouth travel to the heart, kidneys, or liver.

CHAPTER 15   Grooming Your Scottish Terrier

Brushing your dog's teeth with a toothpaste flavored for dogs will make the process more enjoyable for your dog, but you can also invest in dental treats that can help with day-to-day dental care if you don't have the time for daily cleaning. However, daily dental care for your dog can save you a lot of money in the long run.

Cleaning Ears and Eyes

The eyes and ears don't usually get cleaned during baths because these areas are much more sensitive than other parts of the body. You should avoid getting shampoo in your dog's eyes, even if you're using a shampoo labeled as tear-free, and avoid getting water inside your dog's ears as damp ears can breed bacteria and lead to infection.

You can use special wipes to clean your Scottish Terrier's eyes, but any damp cloth will work. Be gentle as you work any gunk out of the corners of her eyes, especially if that gunk has dried into her fur. Check for any unusual discharge during eye cleanings. You should quickly notice what kind of gunk is normal for your dog, but if you're unsure about what's normal, take a picture to share with your vet before cleaning it away.

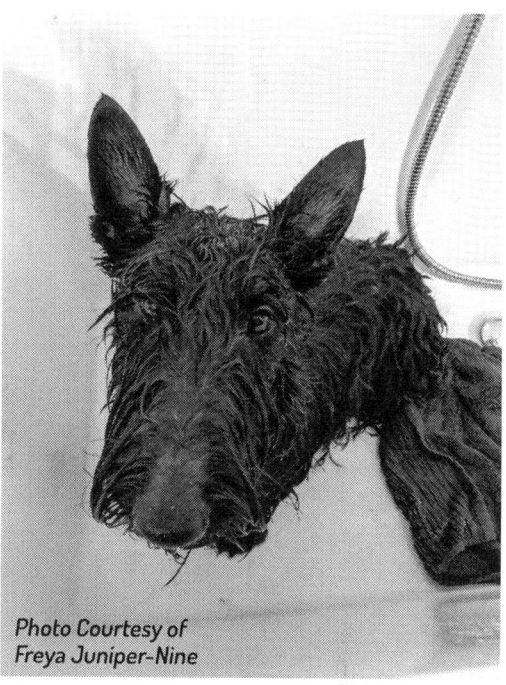

Photo Courtesy of Freya Juniper-Nine

To clean your Scottish Terrier's ears, a simple cotton ball is all you need. You don't want anything smaller to go into your dog's ears and possibly cause damage. Use the cotton ball to gentle swab the inside of the ear, and wipe away any wax or dampness you see. Smell her ear to check for signs of infection. You can also use cotton balls to plug your Scottie's ears during bath time to keep water from entering.

CHAPTER 16
Basic Health Care

Visiting the Vet

Visiting the vet will be a regular occurrence for you and your Scottish Terrier. You should prepare a list of any medications your dog is taking as well as any ailments you've noticed since the last time he's been seen by a licensed professional. You should include the name of the food your dog eats, his bathroom habits, and his activity levels, especially if you're visiting the vet for a specific reason.

Your vet may need a stool sample, which they can take themselves through an uncomfortable process for your pup with a small fee included, so consider calling ahead and planning your dog's bathroom break for a time close to the visit so you can bring along a fresh sample.

Visiting the vet may be stressful if your pet hasn't been to many different places. The vet will smell like many different animals, and there will be other animals around when your dog gets there. Pack some of your dog's favorite toys and treats for the trip to associate the vet with positive experiences before any negative experiences have to occur there.

Fleas and Ticks

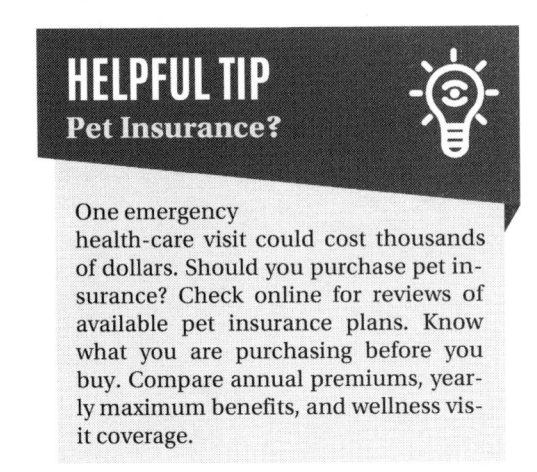

HELPFUL TIP
Pet Insurance?

One emergency health-care visit could cost thousands of dollars. Should you purchase pet insurance? Check online for reviews of available pet insurance plans. Know what you are purchasing before you buy. Compare annual premiums, yearly maximum benefits, and wellness visit coverage.

Fleas and ticks are more prominent in some areas than others. If you live in a warm climate or a highly wooded area, your Scottie may be exposed to fleas and ticks on a regular basis which he may then introduce to your home.

To prevent an infestation, which may take months to eliminate, seek flea and tick treatment. Your veterinarian can sug-

CHAPTER 16 Basic Health Care

Photo Courtesy of Olga Millhouse

gest and provide treatment, but you don't need a prescription to purchase flea treatments. Some treatments work much better than others, depending on the flea prevention chosen types of fleas in your area. Fleas and ticks can pass on diseases and cause skin allergies and excessive itchiness.

Worms and Parasites

Worms and parasites are dangerous to both your dog as well as your family. Dogs can pass on worms in a number of ways including by licking or through their feces. Worms and worm eggs may also drop from your dog's digestive tract onto the floor or cling to the fur on his hindquarters.

Intestinal parasites can cause a host of problems including malnutrition, blood stools, weight loss, vomiting, diarrhea, and more. Dogs can get intestinal parasites from eating infected animals or feces or from licking themselves when infested with fleas.

Treatment includes clearing your home and outside areas of any infected feces or anima corpses that may re-infect your dog as well as treating fleas in your home and yard and on your dog. Your veterinarian can prescribe either a liquid medicine or a pill that will kill adult worms and that needs to be taken again at a later time to kill worms that were still eggs during the first treatment. Your vet can give this medicine to your dog during a visit, or you can do it yourself at home if you're confident you can get your Scottish Terrier to ingest medicine on your own.

Holistic Alternatives

Holistic care focuses on treating the whole body with the aim of maintaining overall health. When using holistic care, diet and exercise are usually the focus of treatment. A holistic veterinarian may advise you to avoid using artificial products on your pet and guide you toward natural alternatives in regard to shampoo, medicine, and food. Massages, acupuncture, and chiropractic are other treatments a holistic vet may suggest. You should consult a licensed veterinarian before taking a holistic approach to your dog's health and treatment.

CHAPTER 16 Basic Health Care

Photo Courtesy of Emily Ashworth

Vaccinations

Dog vaccines are just as important as human vaccines in keeping the population healthy and free of preventable diseases. Vaccinating your dog will help his immune system fight off diseases that may otherwise leave him severely impaired or worse.

Some vaccinations aren't necessary for certain dogs, but your veterinarian will advise you on all the vaccinations available to your dog, which your dog should receive, and the schedule for when your Scottie should receive those vaccinations.

Common vaccinations protect against canine parvovirus, canine distemper, hepatitis, rabies, Bordetella, canine influenza, leptospirosis, and lyme disease.

CHAPTER 16   Basic Health Care

Pet Insurance

Pet insurance allows you to pay a monthly fee that ensures certain treatments or accidents or covered. Without insurance, you could be paying far more than the yearly cost of insurance for a single unexpected or emergency visit.

Certain offices will have their own insurance programs that is applied during the visit, while others will require that you pay out of pocket and get reimbursed for the treatment. Before you purchase any pet insurance, you should be clear about what is and isn't included. You don't want to assume you will be covered for emergencies and realize during the visit that you either don't have the money to treat your beloved pet or that you will have to drain your savings just to do so.

Also be away that there are credit options available specifically for such situations. If you find that you have to pay out of pocket because your pet's insurance plan doesn't cover treatment, don't be afraid to look around for a service that will loan you the money.

Photo Courtesy of Cheryl Fugate

CHAPTER 17
Advanced Scottish Terrier Health and Aging Dog Care

Common Diseases, Conditions, and Genetic Traits in Scottish Terriers

"Bladder cancer is the most prevalent type of cancer found in Scotties. By the time a Scottie is at least five, I would recommend having blood work done, and if necessary an x-ray or ultrasound."

Jane Herron
Herron's Sandhills Scotties

Photo Courtesy of Debbie Jones

CHAPTER 17 Advanced Scottish Terrier Health and Aging Dog Care

Most conditions likely to affect your Scottish Terrier are genetic, although many of those conditions don't present until later in life. Even if you've purchased your Scottish Terrier from a breeder who has screened for certain genetic disorders, your Scottie may develop some of the disorders common to the breed, but testing does lower the chances of these disorders, and not all of them are life-threatening.

> **HELPFUL TIP**
> **Common Disorders**
>
> Most purebreds have a predisposition to certain genetic disorders. Scottish Terriers are considered risky in the health department. Scotties can be prone to bleeding disorders, autoimmune diseases, allergies, and skin conditions. "Scottie Cramp," a neurological disorder found in Scottish Terriers, causes muscles to cramp, making it difficult to walk. Due diligence is required before purchasing your family pet.

Hyperadrenocorticism, also known as Cushing's disease, and hypothyroidism are two disorders that affect the skin and coat of Scottish Terriers. Cushing's disease may lead to bald patches as your Scottie's fur falls out, leaving behind thick and darkened skin. Frequent urination or the outline of a pot belly are signs of Cushing's. Hypothyroidism is an endocrine disorder that occurs when a dog's body doesn't produce enough thyroid hormone. This condition affects weight gain, energy levels, and skin and coat health. Hypothyroidism can cause dandruff, coat loss, and skin infections.

Scotty Cramps is a neuromuscular disorder which confuses brain signals and brings on behavior that resembles cramping and prevents the affected dog from walking correctly. These "cramps" occur after excitement, stress, or exercise, although these cramps aren't like the cramps humans experience. Although the condition doesn't seem painful, it definitely isn't fun for you to watch or for your Scottie to experience since these episodes can look similar to seizures, though they are not, and dogs affected are fine after the episode is over.

Eye diseases such as cataracts and glaucoma may affect your Scottish Terrier as the breed is predisposed to a number of eye diseases with these two being some of the more common diseases. These diseases may occur at any point in your Scottie's life but are more likely in older dogs. After the eye disease is diagnosed, your veterinarian can tell you what treatments are available. The sooner these sometimes-painful eye diseases are diagnosed, the less likely permanent blindness is to occur.

Craniomandibular osteopathy (CMO) is a condition that Scottish Terrier puppies are prone to. This genetic disorder causes abnormal bone growth

Photo Courtesy of Cheryl Fugate

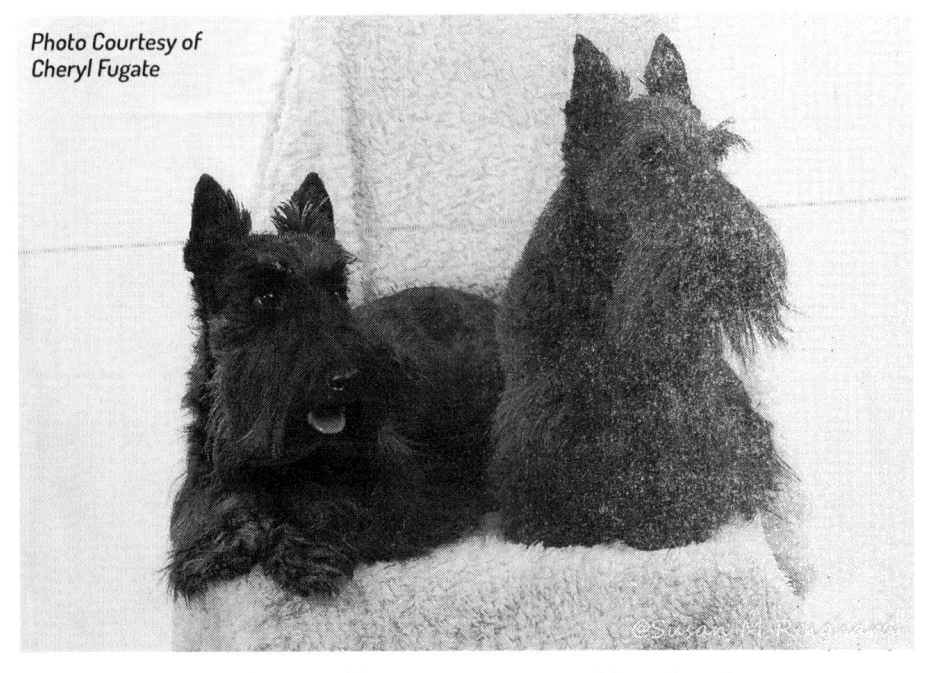

around the jaw of dogs and has no treatment, although pain-management therapy is available. Though this disorder is not deadly and lasts only during the first year of life, the bone growth can result in a wider and thicker jawbone as well as cause pain or limited jaw mobility. This abnormal growth may slow or regress on its own, but if the bone growth is severe enough to restrict eating, surgery may be necessary.

Von Willebrand's disease is a highly dangerous blood-clotting disorder that, thanks to the work of responsible breeders, is less likely to be passed on to future generations of Scottish Terriers. This disorder is caused by a missing or defective Von Willebrand protein that plays a key role in clotting blood. Excessive bleeding may occur even from the smallest of wounds, leading to a dangerous state of low blood pressure if the bleeding isn't able to be stopped. There is no cure for this disorder, and the treatment used to control the bleeding depends on the severity of the condition.

Lymphoma and transitional cell carcinoma are both cancers that are more common in Scottish Terriers than in other dogs. Cancer is the leading cause of death for older dogs, and transitional cell carcinoma is 18 times more likely to affect Scottish Terriers compared to other breeds. Lymphoma is also more likely to occur in the Scottie breed and makes the body produce abnormal white blood cells.

CHAPTER 17 Advanced Scottish Terrier Health and Aging Dog Care

Patellar luxation occurs when the kneecap slips out of its natural position. While this condition can occur from some sort of trauma, it is also genetic. This condition is always painful but severe cases can lead to chronic pain, abnormal knee/leg structure, lameness, and arthritis. Some cases don't require any treatment while others may require surgery to repair the luxated patella.

Hip dysplasia causes the joints of the hips to form improperly. This disease is inherited or can occur during difficult births and can lead to arthritis, lameness, and life-long pain, depending on the severity. Some dogs can live fine with hip dysplasia and only have problems during play or exercise. Others are obviously in pain and walk with an abnormal gait. Improper exercise, weight, and nutrition can make this disease worse. Surgery is a viable treatment for some dogs while others can be treated with diet, exercise, physical therapy, or medication.

Dental disease affects a large number of dogs, regardless of the breed, but Scottish Terriers are more likely than other dogs to develop dental disease. Tartar buildup from the regular ingestion of soft dog foods can lead to dental diseases which, in turn, can affect other areas of the body such as the heart and liver. Without treatment, dental diseases can cause infections that spread from the teeth to the gums and from there to other parts of the body as the infection enters the bloodstream. Dental care for dogs is more widely available than ever before.

Obesity can affect the small-bodied Scottish Terrier greatly. It can seriously weaken joints and make existing joint problems worse, which an older Scottie is already likely to have. Obese Scottish Terriers are also more likely to develop digestive disorders or heart disease, and they will probably suffer from back pain as they struggle to carry more weight than their bodies were meant to. Obesity can be managed with diet and exercise, but it's much harder to manage the weight of an older dog than that of a younger dog, and exercise may be painful or just not help the slowed-down metabolism of an older and overweight dog.

Just because the conditions listed here are common to the Scottish Terrier breed doesn't mean your Scottie will develop them, but realize he is more at risk for certain conditions that you need to prepare yourself for living with and helping him manage.

Though you can't protect your Scottie against every condition he may develop, you can still learn the common conditions as well as the signs and symptoms. If caught early enough, the condition may not be as stressful or intrusive in you and your Scottie's life.

Illness and Injury Prevention

Regardless of how dutiful you are with taking your Scottish Terrier to the veterinarian for checkups and preventive care, your Scottish Terrier can still incur illnesses and injuries. Many illnesses are out of your control such as genetic disorders or conditions your Scottie is predisposed to developing, but you can prevent illnesses involved with your Scottie's environment.

Dogs can and will eat a lot of things they find including dead animals, animal feces, and other things that they may be curious about. Dead animals contain a lot of bacteria that will make your dog sick, and the dead animal may have ingested poison before dying which your dog will then ingest after eating the dead animal. You should regularly clean your yard of your own dog's feces as it will breed bacteria that your dog will be exposed to regularly.

Do not let your Scottie drink from puddles or standing water since these small bodies of water are a breeding ground for bacteria and parasites. Oil, pesticides, and other human-made chemicals may also be present in the runoff from yards and carports.

Heatstroke is likely if you aren't cautious about how long you're exercising your pup during extreme weather. Avoid walks and play during the hottest time of the day, and prevent dehydration by providing plenty of water in such weather.

Injuries your Scottish Terrier is likely to incur can typically be avoided. For instance, having a properly fenced yard will keep your pet from running into a busy street or getting into scraps with other animals. Dog bites can be vicious, and cat bites can easily fester. Other animals may also cause injury to your Scottie's eyes or eyelids.

Inactivity is another cause of injury you can control. Regular exercise can keep your Scottie in shape so he can avoid injuries related to inactivity. Inactivity can lead to obesity which, in turn, can cause other injuries as the body struggles to carry more weight than it's made to.

Inactivity can also lead to destructive behavior which can cause your Scottie to hurt himself. Anxious chewing on unsafe items can cause injury to the mouth or stomach. Inactivity can also cause stiffness and reduce a dog's endurance which can lead to later injury during playtime or other exercises if your dog's muscles haven't been properly warmed up. To prevent inactivity related injuries and illnesses, keep a regular exercise schedule that takes into account your Scottie's recent activity, energy levels, and current health.

CHAPTER 17   Advanced Scottish Terrier Health and Aging Dog Care

Injuries can also happen during regular walks, even if your pup is well-exercised. Hot cement and asphalt can cause blistering on the soft and unprotected pads of your dog's feet during hot summer days. Place your hand on the ground outside before going for walks during the summer. Foot pads can be injured by thorny grass or broken glass; pay attention to the areas around your neighborhood that may have thorny weeds or other painful debris so you know where to avoid walking.

Torn nails can also occur either during walks or during regular play, especially if you haven't kept up with a regular grooming routine. You could also accidentally cut your dog's quick if you haven't trimmed his nails for a while and have let it grow out.

Basics of Senior Dog Care

As your Scottish Terrier begins to age, activities that were once easy will become more and more difficult to perform, and that fact is true for things your Scottie used to do for himself as well as things you used to do for and with him. Not every senior dog will suffer the same deterioration, but there are some common ailments you should prepare yourself for.

Your dog's old age is not an illness, and though it may be burdensome to change your lifestyle and to put in often unpleasant extra work, it's a duty you take on when you first choose to take home your fresh and energetic Scottish Terrier puppy. Old age is a stage of life for both you and your Scottie to experience together, for all the good and bad that this stage holds. Old age is truly the time to show your loyal and steadfast friend how much you've enjoyed and appreciated his companionship over the years.

Your Scottish Terrier, even if he has been relatively healthy through the years, may develop any number of ailments that simply come with living life to its fullest. With any disease or condition developed later in life, many things need to be taken into consideration such as the dog's quality of life, projected years left, and treatment costs. Ultimately, it may all come down to how much pain your furry friend may experience during treatment, if treatment is required or decided upon.

Common Old-age Ailments

Dementia is a sad condition to deal with since your dog may forget many things he's learned and experienced in life, including his time with you and the bond you've formed over the years. Your dog may become aggressive or irritated with humans and animals he was once very friendly with. His sleeping schedule may change or become disrupted, and he may begin passing his bowels in the house since he doesn't remember his training or because he just doesn't have the energy to go outside. Your own observations will be vital in diagnosing dementia; keep a list of changes you've noticed so you can share with your vet.

Dogs are at higher risk for cancer the older they get because their cells don't reproduce as accurately anymore. There are several types of cancers they're at risk for including melanoma and prostate cancer. Scottish Terriers commonly develop bladder cancer, so watch for frequent urination, trouble urinating, and bloody urine.

Kidney failure has similar symptoms as bladder cancer and is another old-age ailment that may affect your older Scottie. The kidneys remove waste from the body, and over the years, the dutiful filtration system may become blocked, damaged, or just weakened from use.

Diabetes is more common in female dogs and is caused by poor insulin production. Symptoms include increased thirst, urination, and weight loss. Diabetes can cause diabetic cataracts in dogs, resulting in blindness as excess glucose in the bloodstream changes the lenses of the eyes. Diet, exercise, and regular injections are common treatments for diabetes.

Arthritis may occur as the cartilage protecting the joints from rubbing together start to wear down over years of natural movement. When the cartilage becomes damaged, your dog's joints may become painfully inflamed, swollen, or stiff. Your Scottie may be reluctant to move with such pain, and treatment includes medication and changes to diet and exercise.

Hormonal changes or a weakened digestive system can cause incontinence in your Scottish Terrier as can prostate disorders, diabetes, and kidney disease. Older dogs are more prone to urinary tract infections, which can also cause urinary incontinence. You may need to purchase puppy pads or doggy diapers for your Scottish Terrier during this time. He may lose his confidence if he constantly has accidents, so be sure to promptly clean any mess and provide clean blankets in his favorite areas. You may need to cut the fur around your Scottie's hindquarters to keep the area clear of feces or urine.

CHAPTER 17 Advanced Scottish Terrier Health and Aging Dog Care

Photo Courtesy of Caroline Reid

Grooming

Grooming is more important than ever at this point in your dog's life. Not only does grooming help older dogs to stay clean and to move around better, but it also helps them to stay comfortable. Older dogs are more sensitive to changes in temperature, especially in areas of extreme heat or cold. Their bodies aren't able to thermoregulate as well as before, and dogs already don't regulate body temperatures as well as humans do.

Since your Scottie can't easily cool himself off, you must make sure his coat doesn't grow to the point that heat is uncomfortably trapped under the fur. This may mean that at a certain point in life, your pup will be sporting a new and much shorter cut. You may even need to increase how often you have his coat cut. Watch for signs of overheating whenever your Scottie's coat is longer. Panting, excessive drooling, and lethargy can indicate that it's time for a new 'do.

Grooming is more difficult for older dogs to endure since they often must stand for long periods of time. Take your older Scottie's comfort into consideration by breaking up grooming sessions into smaller, more frequent sessions. Consider taking breaks to massage your Scottie's sore muscles during these sessions, and avoid startling your older dog.

Keep nails short to avoid them tearing or catching on things, and trim down the hair around the pads of your Scottie's feet to ensure he has sufficient traction as he walks. Frequent teeth cleaning can help reduce dental diseases. Older dogs are more prone to ear infections, so check ears daily, and clean them frequently. Older dogs may require more baths, and you should be sure to keep your Scottie warm right after a bath to prevent a drastic change in temperature as he begins cooling down from a warm bath.

Nutrition

Since your Scottish Terrier is older now, his body won't work as well as it did when it was younger, including his digestive system. A higher-quality diet with ingredients in their more natural forms will allow your older Scottie to absorb nutrients better. Your veterinarian can help you to choose an appropriate senior dog food for your Scottish Terrier's specific needs.

A food that is lower in calories is also important since older dogs are less likely to be active and suffer from higher rates of obesity. Mobility issues such as arthritis and other joint pain will lessen activity even more, making weight-loss attempts harder than they would have been when your Scottish Terrier was in his prime.

CHAPTER 17   Advanced Scottish Terrier Health and Aging Dog Care

Exercise

While diet does play an important role in your senior dog's health, regular movement is equally important not only for weight management and joint health but also your Scottie's mental sharpness.

Exercise shouldn't be as long or as intense as it was when your dog was younger, but all dogs need activity to maintain energy reserves, muscle strength, and mental health. Dogs are outdoor animals, and the lifestyle that the modern dog leads alongside humans already doesn't offer the same mental stimulation that their ancestors had. Regular exercise, play, and walks can encourage calmness and reduce anxiety.

Additionally, even a simple walk is enough to fire off neurons in your Scottie's brain. A walk introduces new smells, sounds, places, and people. He's definitely explored all there is to explore in his home, so presenting him with something new can help his older brain make new connections. Walks also serve as bonding time, even if you two already have a strong bond. A walk will remind your older Scottish Terrier that he's still as important to you as he always has been.

When It's Time to Say Goodbye

Humans know that they will outlive their animal companions, but this knowledge often doesn't prepare anyone for the reality of losing a trusted friend and family member.

It may be hard to accept when it's time to say goodbye, especially if you're dedicated to taking care of your Scottie no matter how many ailments he may have, especially if he still seems happy to enjoy life with you. Unfortunately, we must put aside personal selfishness and realize that our pets' quality of life is more important than the comfort that their presence provides us.

There are many signs that your Scottish Terrier is ready to pass on, and you may be instinctively aware of what these signs mean. Lethargy and disinterest in the things that once made them happy is one sign that the dying process has begun. Your dog's body is preparing itself for death by reducing the amount of resources it uses. As such, he will stop eating and drinking, even if you're offering him his favorite treats. Other health issues can cause similar symptoms, so be sure to take your pet to the vet for confirmation if you suspect death is near.

Photo Courtesy of
Allyson Albinson

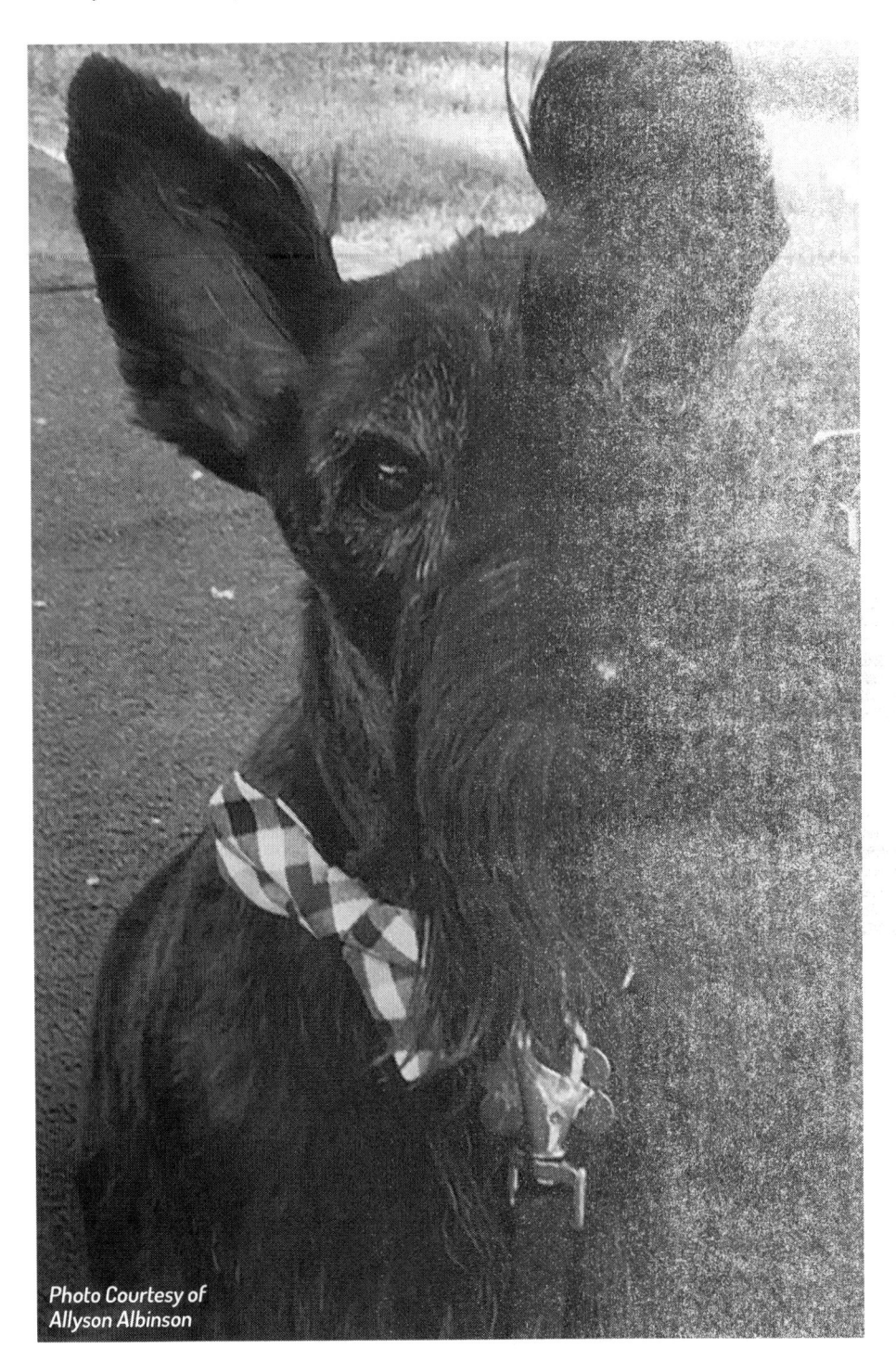

CHAPTER 17   Advanced Scottish Terrier Health and Aging Dog Care

Besides disinterest, your Scottish Terrier may lose coordination and wobble or convulse. Such behavior may be distressing to both you and your friend, so don't be surprised if he decides to find a spot to lie in for long periods of time.

Your Scottish Terrier may know when his time is coming and will search you out for comfort. If this scenario does happen, you should stay with your dog and be calm and reassuring. Though it is stressful for you to lose your companion, you don't want to transfer your own stress to your dog during his last moments.

Of course, you don't need to wait until your Scottish Terrier has gone through the more common signs of close death. Other symptoms of death such as incontinence and labored breathing can be an indication that it's time for veterinarian-assisted death, which will be much more peaceful and will allow you and your Scottish Terrier to properly say goodbye before the scheduled appointment.

You can schedule a house call if your local vet provides that service and you want your friend to pass in a familiar place, and you can also make the trip to the vet if you think you need the vet to handle burials and they offer such a service.

Although losing such a close friend is heartbreaking and painful, you must remember that you have had a long life with your friend, and he surely appreciates all the love, time, and attention that you provided him over the years.

Made in United States
Orlando, FL
16 July 2024